MW01697959

FROM THE WISTARIA BUSH

FROM THE WISTARIA BUSH
VANYA LOWRY
AUCKLAND UNIVERSITY PRESS
aup

First published 2001

Auckland University Press
University of Auckland
Private Bag 92019
Auckland
New Zealand
http://www.auckland.ac.nz/aup

ISBN 1 86940 256 1

Publication is assisted by creative nz
Arts Council of New Zealand Toi Aotearoa

Cover design by Christine Hansen
Front cover illustration: Vanya Lowry, 'From the Wistaria Bush'
Back cover photograph: Vanya graduating Dip. Fine Arts, 1967. Simon Buis

Printed by Astra Print Ltd, Wellington

NATIONAL LIBRARY OF NEW ZEALAND CATALOGUING-IN-PUBLICATION DATA

Lowry, Vanya.
From the wistaria bush / by Vanya Lowry. 1st ed.
Includes bibliographical references.
ISBN: 1-86940-256-1
1. Lowry, Bob. 2. Lowry, Vanya — Family. 3. Lowry family.
4. Printers — New Zealand — Auckland.
I. Title.
686.2092—dc 21

BOB, VANYA, IRENE, ROBIN, JUDY, POP. AT THE WADE

This book is dedicated to: the memory of my late mother Irene and father Bob, and my grandparents; to my two dear sons, George Port and Oliver McWilliams, and my delightful daughter, Amber, who patiently taught me to use the Apple Mac and got me seriously started; and to my aunts Althea and Iris, my friends and my sisters who shared stories, poems, photographs and recipes with me, especially little sister Brigid, who inspired by beating me to it. With love.

VINEGAR
Honey
Mustard
MILK
OIL
Apple & Lime
Marmalade
December '73
CAPERS
HONEY
Lemon
Cheese
Tamarillo
Chutney
Jan '74
Passionfruit Cheese

CONTENTS

PROLOGUE

FROM THE WISTARIA bush I can see the lit rooms of the house across the chequered patio. Here I crouch in my favourite hideaway, this Friday night in early summer.

These choking clusters of heavy-scented purple flowers tickle my nose so I desperately want to sneeze, but must not. How cold it is out here under the wistaria bush, how scary.

Daddy is roaring through the lit-up empty rooms, cursing, calling for Mummy, who went out an hour ago, probably for a walk to the phone-box down at Royal Oak to call a secret friend for sympathy.

My big sisters, they too are hiding somewhere in the moonlit garden. With luck, Daddy will discover our three empty beds and stomp off, muttering, to fall snoring into his own.

With luck, Mummy won't disturb him when she comes creeping home and we won't hear those high screams like a cat in the night and have to rush through the dark house to rescue our mother from strangling.

And in the morning Daddy may not have to ask what happened in the night, remembering nothing. He will pick Mummy a little bunch of wild violets from the cracks in the path while he waits for the jug to boil so he can take her a nice cup of tea in bed.

'I am a dark river . . .', he will tell her, as if that's any excuse. And once again Mummy will think of leaving him, and taking us kids, but because of us kids, she will stay and give him one more chance.

Irene: A study by Clifton Firth

VANYA'S BATH IN WATER SCARCITY

PART ONE:
FROM THE WISTARIA BUSH

Dad sent this from New Caledonia

↑ Army Headquarters

Group of Black Debutantes Presented to His Excellency on an island in the Northern Solomons.

From RIGHT to Left:

Nobblers, Bobblers, Wobblers, Droopers,

Super-Droopers, Too Young and Razor Strops.

IRENE, BOB & LITTLE PUDDING

YOU COULD SAY my life actually began in Wellington, to an inauspicious start, when a friend of student Irene Cornes informed her, 'Bob Lowry's coming, whatever you do don't trust him with money!' If only she had heeded this good advice! But now, a tired old lady 'knocking on heaven's door', I look back and my childhood seems one continuous party weekend in The Party House. But that can't be right. Can it?

Anyway, it's our house that's the hero of this story, the house Irene and her handsome Bob bought together in the late 1930s, the sprawling old trollop of a place on the slopes of One Tree Hill beside Cornwall Park. Here is where I spent the first twenty years of my life.

Two daughters were born before I was conceived, which happy event took place, I like to think, when Irene was taken on the back of a friend's motorbike for a quick visit to Bob stationed at the Ardmore Army Training Camp. My father would not meet me until I was ten months old. But at my birth he had not expected a miracle, although hopeful of a son this time, to be printing apprentice and garden helper. So he sent suggestions such as 'Micheline' and 'Nicolette' from New Caledonia, where he was having a marvellous war, printing the Forces newspaper, and gathering delicious tropical fruit from the roadsides ripe for the plucking. So my mother, suspecting that these were the names of dusky French girlfriends, decided to name me after Chekhov's famous uncle and that was that.

Well, of course, at first my father resented me for waking in the night hungrily crying for my mother's attention when he wanted her all to himself. But one day he saw me come to a barrier gate on the verandah, and with great determination climb over it. Then he knew I was definitely a chip off the old block, and loved me. At first he called me his 'Little Pudding', probably from 'Warnya-Tiny-Pudding' as his apprentice Robin Lush fondly called me, but so rapidly did I thrive that I soon became known as just 'Pudding'. Friend Bill Anso called me 'Sunshine-on-a-rainy-day'. Friend Pat Dobbie called me 'Pungiau', from a favourite opera. But to my little friends Jammy and Jojo from next door I was always Vanna, and I liked that best.

MERRY CHRISTMAS · HAPPY NEW YEAR

FROM THE LOWRY FAMILY

32 GLADWIN RD · EPSOM · AUCKLAND

SISTERS & PUSSYCATS

CURLED UP ON my bed reading a super library book I don't hear my mother the first time she calls me to set the table. She has to come to the other end of the house and get me. She seems nervous dishing dinner, clumsily dropping the pot of hot spuds into the sink when she pours away the water. She has scalded her hands, but I know for sure something else must be up because she uses her very worst swear word. So I go on silently setting knives in place on the right and forks on the left, wondering whether to put out spoons as well for pudding, but dare not ask. My mother takes a gulp of her red wine then sighs a long sigh before sloshing a little top milk into the buttered spuds and mashing them. She ladles out two sausages for each plate, plus a dollop of silverbeet and two dollops of mash, and puts my father's plate over a pot of water on the stove to keep warm, for as usual on a Friday night he's late home.

'Call your sisters, Vanna,' says my mother, so I go to the door of the Bedroom Wing and yell, 'Come and ge-e-et it!' Soon Robin, Judy and I are seated around the table, our mother at one end and only our father's seat empty at the other. A liberal slosh of tomato sauce and I begin tucking into my favourite meal of burst snarlers, mash and silverbeet, oblivious to my sisters chattering on about their day. But halfway through the meal my mother blurts it out.

'Girls . . . I've got something exciting to tell you. Bob and I . . . that is . . . I mean . . . well, how would you like a new baby brother — or sister?'

'*What*!' So she's giving Daddy another chance?

'I thought forty was too old, Mother?'

'When's the baby due? It might be a brother at last.'

'Who will it be named after? Can I be godmother to it, Mummy, please?'

We're all so rapt, so excited, we can barely finish our meal. But our mother has made a fudge pudding for after, which is also a favourite of mine, so I manage somehow. Then she says she has to go out for a little walk to clear her head, and we're all to get the dishes done, homework finished, and get ourselves off to bed at a reasonable hour, okay?

BUT I AM the trees. And I shall stand up strong and tall and beautiful, learning the never-ceasing wonders of the sky. I shall feel the loving clasp of the good earth at my roots, shall stretch out these brown arms and twisted fingers, and, as the cool air wraps me round, know that there is no kiss like the kiss of the wind. I too shall feel life moving, the sap within my bark, and dear chattering birds among my branches. I shall learn wisdom from the noises of the day. And in the night the dreams will come, down the long corridor slowly to my curtained cubicle, and cold moonlight through the windows will cut that little room into splinters, yes, splinters of sharp air, and the witch hiding behind the curtain will give it a twitch somewhere beyond these tightly closed eyes. How loud the house is with the creaking of boards and witch whisperings, how long the black velvet night in that huge gum tree looming outside my window, where dark shapes of monsters squat, waiting to swoop down and gobble me up. The house trembles and is small under its cloak of darkness as I lie waiting for the lovely rooster morning. It must easily be midnight when I start dreaming I'm this tender little witch stuck in some horrible world where you never do anything, you only have things done to you. And from this weird place I must escape, whizzing out the window on my vacuum-cleaner, for I'm a modern witch, flying free up and away above the houses, streets and harbours, away beyond dreaming, till the glad morning.

And somehow the glad morning always comes, so I will get up, pulling on my old white shorts and stripy T-shirt. I will know I've been out flying, for my head was burrowed down the foot of the bed and my feet were sleeping on the pillow! On my way to the kitchen I stop in the lower bathroom for a quick face-wash in the corners of sleep-encrusted eyes.

Sitting on the loo, I smile at the sight of the lifesize statue of Venus that my loopy sister Robin, 'the artistic one', has painted all over with red and green measle spots. The poor headless armless footless thing looks so jolly cold. But dead funny, I reckon.

In the kitchen nobody is about but dancing sunlight is caught in coloured bottles along the window sill. There are good smells of toast and marmalade, and my father's fry-up of scrambled egg, bacon and onions. Helping myself to some breakfast, I take it out on the sunny patio, where after a while our tomcat, Ponsonby, comes purring hungrily around my feet. So I feed him the last of my Weetbix, though he would prefer winter's porridge. Now he leaps onto my lap for stroking and I search his thick black fur for fleas, which I like to crunch between two thumbnails.

I dress Ponsy in my doll's red spotty dress with matching hanky around his neck, and push him in the cane pram along the paths till he manages to wriggle out to go and find his faithful little tortoiseshell wife, Remuera. I chase butterflies around the lawn with the butterfly net, for in a good mood my father will pay a penny for ten dead cabbage-whites, and sixpence will get me into the Saturday matinee at the Regent Epsom — the Marx Brothers, Charlie Chaplin, Spider Woman! I will be able to go with Jammy and Jojo when they ask me. Ponsy and Remuera joyously join in, chasing me and butterflies around in circles. When we've done that I will pick some flowers and listen to their secrets. Shadows come and go on the terrace, where I play hopscotch and black crickets jump and keen their rasping summer song.

Now Judy comes out onto the terrace with a chair, followed by Robin with tea towel and scissors and pudding-basin and a comb for getting out the knots. So my big bossy sister proceeds to trim Judy's sunbleached mop, and I run and hide among the summery branches of the plum tree to avoid a haircut and Robin's bad-tempered morning breath which she uses to blow the tickly bits off your face.

AT THE PARTY HOUSE

IN THE GARDEN now, I can see the comforting sight of my father at the back door pulling on his old mud-caked gardening shoes. Through dappled leaves I watch him in his bright Hawaiian shirt and baggy khaki shorts bending to hoe between his rows of vegetables. Through the kitchen window I can see my mother coming out to drink her fourth cup of tea, light a fag and turn the radio on for morning classics.

Then the music is earth, is air, is fire, this wild music calling me, calling me. So I climb down the tree and run through the French doors to the Big Room, where the music is loud and the floor is so wide, around and around I go, up and down, in and out, and wheee, I'm a flame dancing, a butterfly, a wisp, a leaf in the wind, Tzena Tzena Tzena!

But now I'm puffed and the half-finished library book on my bedside chair is calling me, so I go and snuggle down on my bed to read till my mother calls us all to lunch. She has cooked the big pot of sweetcorn my father proudly brought in from the garden. When we've finished chomping into the sweet cobs with salty butter dripping down our chins and arms, my father, beaming expansively, says there's to be a party tonight, in honour of the expected baby and also because his poet friend Jim happens to be visiting from the south. Robin is to do the flower arranging, while we younger kids can help Irene with her famous pies, and polish the floor of the Big Room, ready for the dancing.

'I bags do the floor, Daddy!' I chirp quickly. 'I'll find Jammy or Jojo to help me!' My father nods okay and goes on, 'So, Juju-a-puju, will you help Irene bake dem famous golden pies?' So of course Judy agrees to help with the baking, after she has done her ballet practice, that is, and off she goes to her barre beside her cubicle. First position, second position, third position, fourth and fifth, *plié* and *jeté* and *pas de chat*. . . .

'Here's some silverbeet, Irene, and have you got a spare fag?' asks my father at the kitchen door a little later.

'My last one,' mutters my mother, leaning against the cool sink-bench, taking a last drag before stubbing it out in one of the scallop shells used as ashtrays.

'Where's that old Pudding?' I hear my father ask. 'I'll send her along to the Tea Kiosk for some more, eh?'

'You can't send her, they don't sell to nine-year-olds,' says Robin, helping herself to several Weetbix with top milk and lots of brown sugar. 'They won't even let me have any.'

'And since when have you been smoking, madam?' frowns my mother.

'Since never, Mother, but I tried buying some there once, just to get in good with the Bullyboys. . . .'

Leaving my mother and Robin arguing over the Bullyboys, my father comes out calling me, but already I'm slithering down the mossy trunk of the plum tree, where I've been hiding out reading, to take the coins — 'One shilling and threepence, which buys ten De Reszke,' I'm instructed. Hopping on my little bike, I pedal along beside low stone walls, through the great oaks, over the cattlestop past the Scout Hall, up the little hill between whispering elms and silvery olive grove, whizzing down the other side to rattle over the next

By Eric Lee-Johnson

cattlestop, past Moreton Bay figs and Acacia Cottage, stopping beside the ice-cream and tobacco shop at the Tea Kiosk.

'Here's one an' frippence for ten De Reszke, please,' I say boldly to the big man glaring down at me, for my bike has fallen over where I parked it, crashing into his flower garden.

'No way, laddie!' he growls.

'But it's for my Daddy, he'll growl at me if I don't bring 'em,' I protest, not bothering to correct him on the 'laddie' bit in my more immediate distress.

'Then go home and tell your Daddy if he needs ten De Reszke to come and purchase them himself because we don't sell to little boys like you!'

'But . . . but he's too busy, sir. . . .'

'Then get him to write a note for you, authorising it. Now get your bike out of my marigold border and *scat*!'

I bike home and tell my father what the Mean Man said. So he scribbles a note for me to take back, on his official letterhead paper with the date and everything. Robin, listening as she reads at the kitchen table over her leisurely Weetbix, suggests I change out of my shorts and T-shirt into my prettiest summer dress and dainty shoes, and even offers to brush my tousled hair, tying it up with a big pink ribbon, to give the Mean Man a surprise.

You should see the look on his face when I roll up there and hand him the note! On the way back, with the slim red pack of fags safely in my basket, I notice something wonderful lying in the gutter. It's a ten-shilling note, a fortune! When I get home I hand my father his fags, and can't help showing the money I found. At once my father claims it, saying he lost a ten-shilling note coming home along the Park last night, even turning out his pocket to show a bloody great hole in it.

So not only do I believe him and hand over the money, but I also offer to fix the hole in his pocket, and on Sunday night agree to iron his shirts for the following week as usual. That's the sort of charmer he is, the sort of love and forgiveness he inspires. And that's how I will always explain it, when people don't understand and ask why we children and my mother stayed with him so long, all those years he'd get so bad-tempered when things weren't going his way, like a spoilt little boy who never grew up. . . .

WHEN 'ROBIN-A-BOBBIN' remembers that she has to do her piano practice, scales and 'Rondo alla Turca' and 'Für Elise' (till it gets to the tricky bit), she finds that the piano is out of tune, so my mother calls the blind piano-tuner, whose daughter luckily can drive him straight over. And he plays around on the keys looking thoughtful, then takes the back off the piano, an upright Rose made in India, exposing the innards. There he finds a dead mouse, which could have had something to do with it. My mother says it's a good thing the mouse wasn't there that time the piano was played by a famous pianist called Lili Kraus. My father had printed the programmes for her concert tour, and she liked them very much so she came around to meet him. When she arrived, the first thing my father asked Lili to play was a favourite song of his, 'She wheels her wheelbarrer / Through streets broad and narrer, / Crying "Cockles and mussels, / Alive, alive-oh" ', and he'd taken a recording of my mother warbling alongside, which made her blench every time she thought of it.

Before leaving to get the grog from Kumeu, my father has given my mother the list of people she is *not* to phone and invite, those who have fallen foul of him over money or deadlines. But when she has finished calling all their other friends, has rolled out the pastry and is busy crying into the chopped onions, a proscribed poet called Keith phones to wheedle an invite, having heard about the party over the grapevine. And his pleading is successful, for as usual my mother will manage to sort it out with my father on his return from the vineyards. Keith will be pushing his luck a bit, though, when he turns up wearing a bright red shirt!

But, while Daddy is away, the mice will play, or at least relax a bit. After a spell on the loo, reading about this magical ship that could fly, I start feeling thirsty, so go out into the garden to see if there are any grapefruit ripe. Robin, bored with piano scales and 'Für Elise' already, is out there picking irises.

She's telling me about one time our Aunty Iris went and got married, and a certain friend, who was sort of in love with our aunty, was so upset he went around our garden slashing the heads off all the irises, when my best friend Jojo comes through the hole in our overgrown hedge.

'Hiya, Jojo, wanna help me polish the floors for the dancing tonight?'

'Yeah, I would, Vanna, but Nan says your father's just a drunken sot an' I'm not allowed to play with you any more so I jus' came over to tell you that.' But the hell with Nan! Forgetting the grapefruit drink, I tell Jojo that what the eye doesn't see the heart doesn't grieve over. So he and I go searching through the chaos of our shed and find all sorts of interesting and useful things there, and we sample sweet old honey from a rusty tin left over from my parents' honeymead experiment. Eventually we find the old grater and the lump of beeswax and a good big sack for Jojo to sit on while I drag him around the floor to get a good shine on for the dancing.

Mead

(Recipe : Norah Dumble)

Weather must be warm. Ideal temp. 70°-80° F.
Must not be under 65° F.
To 1 gallon of water use 2lbs. honey.
These ripe, fresh fruits may be used (squashed)
plums; blackberries; apricots; — in
quantity of 3lbs to 1 gallon water.
If apples are used - use slightly more.
Raisins:- 1lb. to 1 gallon water.
Not recommended — Peaches or Pears.
Extra fruit gives fruit flavour and quicker ferment.
Do not at any stage use metal utensils.

Put mixture in open wooden tub or barrel.
Allow to ferment 10-14 days. Maximum ferment
is reached in 5-7 days. After 10-14 days
it starts subsiding.
A press avoids waste, but if press is
not obtainable, strain through burlap or hessian
or sacking.
Have a cask, placed horizontally, with hole
in side, and fill up to hole with fluid.
Must be kept full daily. Add water
if necessary.
When fermentation slows down, [approximately
3 months, depending on weather] put wooden
bung lightly in hole to exclude air.

When weather gets colder and fermentation ceases, tap bung in.
During the coldest month that fermentation has ceased, syphon fluid off, starting from the centre of the fluid, and using a rubber pipe, push tube slowly down. Stop syphoning when sediment is reached. Wash out sediment thoroughly. Rinse cask three times. Return mead to cask. Fill cask with water and leave until weather is warmer - over 65°.

Make separate mixture.

To each 10 gallons mead use 1-1½ lbs. honey and 1lb. raisins or other fruit.
If too much honey is used - bottles will burst. If too little is used there is less fizz.
Mix with ½ gallon of water, or according to topping space in barrel. Put in separate cask or jars till fizzing well, strain.

Add this mixture to mead and leave bung on it. Watch daily until white mountain of bubbles rise over bung hole [about 1 week] Then bottle. Use beer bottles with crown caps & use capping machine. Keep six weeks before drinking. Good LUCK!

OFF THE BIG Room, the lower door leads to a tiny hall in the Bedroom Wing. The lower bathroom leads off this hallway beside the front door, which is rarely used. First-time visitors coming up the winding track from the street will sometimes cross to the front door by mistake, past the giant gum tree, past wild artichokes yellow-flowering under the clump of bay trees, over the lush boggy 'lawn' above the septic tank. A banana-passionfruit vine twines tender tendrils around the front door, and if the strangers are lucky on this busy Saturday one of us may happen to hear the knocking and will come and let them in. Straight ahead they will see the open linen cupboard with its piles of mangy old army blankets, grey with a red stripe, and turned sheets, and pillow-cases made from old shirts, also a bag of old clothes for the jumble sale, another of remnants for school patchwork projects, and one of rags for washing windows, for which we kids get paid a penny a pane — and I have to tell you it is a house of *very* many windows.

To the left of this rarely used front door are the sleeping cubicles, the second and third of which are mine and Judy's. The large end room is Robin's; being the eldest she always gets the biggest and best of everything. Each of the four cubicles has back windows opening onto the garden, overlooking a snow-ball bush, white may, a pale camellia, to views of Manukau Harbour beyond. Each contains a single bed, bedside chair, small numdah rug, a built-in desk and curtained wardrobe. Once, in her wardrobe, during a game of Truth or Dare, Judy kissed a boy called Gregor a hundred times. Whatever happened to Gregor, anyway?

Along the right of the wooden-floored corridor, French doors lead out onto the lawn, citrus trees and patio beside the wistaria bush, where in summer raggedy daisies grow like giant poached eggs, loud with bees. On the left the concrete path gives way to a dirt track which leads around the big bedroom. In here Robin has to pick her way across the floor through her messes of grubby clothes, half-finished canvases, topless tubes of paint, paint-smeared easel, bottles of turps and linseed oil, painty rags, mouldy old applecores and left-over snacks. Her side window gives onto the path between the azalea bush and my mother's rockery with its succulents and little pink-tipped and yellow daisies. Through this window Robin has taken every opportunity to escape and go down the graveyard with *some boy*, which will end in *no good*.

'One day, my girl, you'll get yourself into *trouble*!' roared my father one time after Robin got caught sneaking out. She'd thrown a tantrum, thrown her dinner at the wall and shut herself in her bedroom to sulk. But actually I can hardly *wait* till, in trouble, she has to leave home and get *married*, and then the room will be Judy's, and when *she* leaves to get married, it will be mine, all *mine*!

The big bedroom

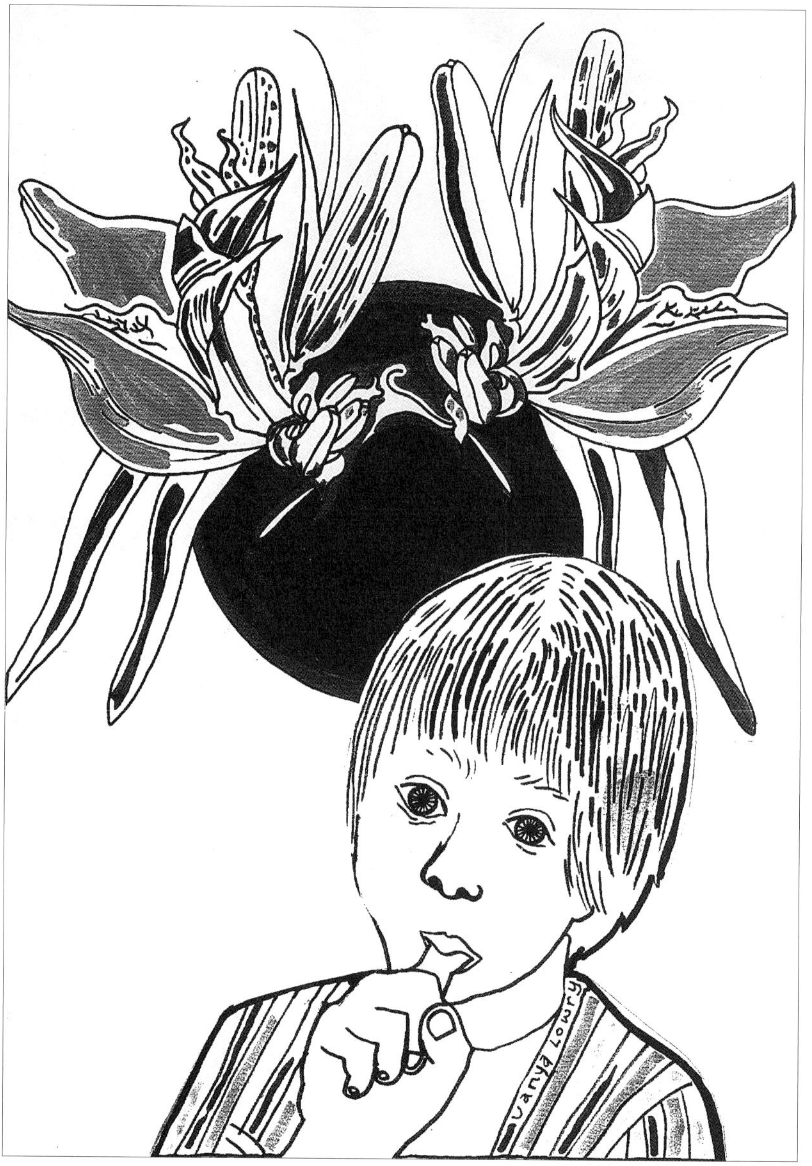
Vanya Lowry

VISITING FRANK SARGESON

ON THIS SATURDAY afternoon my cheerful old friend the Pedlar man turns up with his sugarbag full of tinned pineapple for supper, pineapple-chunk lollies for my sisters, and for me (his 'Biscotti') a bag of broken biscuits and my favourite Juicyfruit gum. He offers to help by scything 'the lawns' or doing a spot of weeding, but my mother remembers the time he completely scythed away (thinking it a rather flourishing weed!) some precious plant she'd been nurturing from a cutting. She suggests, 'Why don't you take Vanna for a nice ride in the ferry over to Esmonde Road to visit Frank, deliver these proofs from Bob? It'd be a big help and keep you both out of mischief for the afternoon.'

Of course, sometimes he and I took the mischief with us, for he had a way of hoisting me on his shoulders to stride down the street. Once in Queen Street I'd left a wake of destruction behind as I joyously snatched the hats off passers-by to throw in the air! Another time, when I was just three, he'd had to take me into the men's loo so I didn't pee my pants. An irate social worker, spotting this, waited outside, ropable about 'What the little girl might have seen!' So the Pedlar man calmly explained I'd just been potty-trained, and should I have been allowed to wet my pants? Here was my mother's phone number for her to check it out. Anyway, all I'd seen was this white porcelain *thingy* along one wall with little waterfalls that you never saw in the Ladies.

At Esmonde Road, Frank's gnomish figure, specs glinting, greets us at the shack door. Quizzically he tilts his head.

'Ah, here's the little girl with the gin-drinker's voice!' he jokes. 'And good old Bill, of course. Well, come in, come in. Oh splendid, you've brought those proofs at last . . . nice surprise. Mind the broom handle there, girl. I'll just shift these papers off the . . . well well, have a bar-stool, Bill, I was just going to make a cuppa. I reckon you won't say no, will you?'

While Frank bustles about preparing a pot of tea, me and my old Pedlar man make ourselves at home. In Frank's little bach the walls seem held up by bookshelves overflowing with heaps and heaps of books, mainly orange Penguins, with Keith Patterson paintings filling in any spaces. Vines come tendriling in the windows of the loo, where I always go as soon as we arrive. Frank's extra-low wooden throne is my favourite place to sit and watch a spider spinning its web to catch a fly for lunch.

And after my pee, daydreaming, I hear from the kitchen Frank's voice asking, 'Does she still think she's a pussycat?' My Old Man laughs and replies, 'We're working on it. And of course she's still my Sunshine-on-a-rainy-day!' Coming back, I'm pleased to find Frank has placed my usual saucer of milk on the hearth among the dried yellow gourds. I lap it up with my rough pink tongue and, when I've finished, curl up purring on the lumpy sofa listening to the Old Man telling Frank a funny story about how he dug this bomb shelter, and then filled it in again. Puckishly Frank laughs, and then suggests that the Old Man did it to escape the house and avoid the sharp tongue of his little Londoner wife, Ruby, who'd never recovered from the hard labour of giving birth to one of their two daughters, all alone on the dirt floor of their gum-digger's tent.

The Old Man pours some tea into his saucer to cool it, then slurps it up contentedly while they start talking about boring old compost heaps and garden pests, and about this story collection the Old Man brought out, which my father printed, about Biscotti and Caramelle, in which Carolyn Dobbie played Caramelle while I was the boy, Biscotti! In the middle of this Kevin the paper-boy clumps in the back door, waving a newspaper and calling, 'Hey, Frank, did you see this?' There on the front page is a blurry photo of Frank in an old raincoat and knapsack, with his neatly pointed beard and black beret, and the headline 'Unknown Writer Wins Prize'.

'Well, I'll be damned!' exclaims my Old Man. 'You cunning old beggar ... I'll be blowed!'

And Frank smirks modestly, unable to contain his glee. 'Ah well, you know how it is ... Maybe the goddam neighbours will forgive me the overgrown hedge and fibro shack now — and the fact that young Kevin here lets me see their newspaper before delivering it, eh Kevin!'

When all the excitement dies down, Frank picks some veg to make one of his famous stews and the Old Man pours Lemora into Vegemite glasses to celebrate. With my chin resting on the smooth wooden bench I watch Frank tenderly chopping up green peppers, onions, aubergines and tomatoes. He sizzles them into the pan, and I sniff the friendly smells of stew and crusty brown bread which the Old Man is cutting into thick slabs. 'Make yourself useful, girl, here's the butter and the knife.'

Frank asks if we had any good adventures this time on the way over.

'Ooh yes, today we went down the engine room of the *Kestrel* and saw all these huge shiny throbbing piss—piss—piss. . . .'

'Pistons, Pussycat, rods and pistons,' reminds the Old Man, 'and they were pumping away and well-oiled as greased lightning, eh! And guess who we saw down there, Frank, your old friend Rex Fair . . .'

'Don't mention that old hypocrite's name to me!' interrupts Frank, looking cross and swiftly changing the subject. 'So, girl, what was the best time you've had with your Old Man?' He hands me the tea-towel as he begins washing up the lunch dishes so as not to encourage blowflies, while the Old Man takes Frank's big spade and goes out, cheerfully whistling through his false teeth, to clear a weedy corner ready for planting.

I remember one time on the way home from Taupaki, or was it Otorohanga, when my Old Man had to fell a tree to make a bridge across a stream for a short cut so we wouldn't miss our train, and while waiting I'd rolled around on the bank, crushing buttercups, then had to run through the green and gold paddock holding on to my Old Man's hand for dear life as the train whistle came closer and closer. . . .

'Frosty place, Otorohanga,' remarks Frank, wiping his sudsy hands on a smelly old tea-towel. He gives me a couple of paper bags to pick aubergines and capsicums for my dear mother, things that don't grow at our place. Then, leading me out into the sunny garden, Frank asks if I have thought of writing down the little story about the buttercup field, so I tell him that as a matter of fact I *did* send several stories off to the Children's Page but haven't heard back. Frank settles himself on the bench to read in the shade of the grapevine. A cat appears from under the shack to nuzzle up, purring on his knee.

After checking to see if any loquats are ripe, I thread my way through corn, tomato and bean rows and settle down to watch the Old Man at his digging. As he turns spadefuls of rich wormy earth, sweat rolls down his bronzed naked torso into his khaki shorts, which are held up with a piece of twine.

'Hey, girl with the gin-drinker's voice,' I hear Frank calling. My Old Man reckons it must be time for a spell and goes to get a drink of water from the garden tap, and I go over to Frank, who is regally waving the newspaper at me. 'Or should I say *budding author*?'

'What, what?' I stammer. It's the Children's Page, they've used one of my stories. Oh bliss, oh fame, oh help! It's the one about the boy who went away to war and came back to his secret mountain pool afterwards to play his pipe, his happy pipe. Frank and the Old Man pronounce it a damn good little piece, for a first try. 'Maybe I'll be a writer when I grow up, like you.'

'What's this? I thought Pussycat was never going to grow up, like Peter Pan. Has Pussycat changed her mind now, then?' And the Old Man ruffles my hair with his huge dirt-ingrained paw, and suggests an ice-cream might be a fitting celebration of this promising start to my career. He takes his tobacco tin from a deep pocket, unravels the rubber bands holding it closed, and brings out some coins from his stash. 'Off you go . . . And remember not to accept lollies from strange old men, will you?', giggling at his own little joke.

'And while you're there buy two copies of the paper, eh girl?' says Frank, forking out some more coins. 'And you'll be needing paste and a scrapbook as well for all the press clippings you'll be wanting to save . . . oh, and stuff this newspaper in the neighbour's letterbox on your way past, will you?'

In a contented bee-loud haze I happily paste my first-ever *press clipping* into my very first scrapbook, and gloat over it. My funny old friend Frank is still chortling over his newspaper story about the 'Unknown Writer' as he comes through the hole in his hedge to see us off. '"Unknown Writer reckons winning will make no difference to his lifestyle. . . ." Oh sure, that'll be the day! After paying all the bills I fully intend to get Haydn to build on another room for my dear friends to stay — and maybe a sunporch as well, eh?'

My Old Man lifts me up on his shoulders, ordering me to hold tight to his silver mane of hair. Then, with my knees in the way, he gives a clumsy hug to Frank, who looks wistful and asks, 'Are you sure you won't change your mind, m'dear?' and I feel a shuddering across the Old Man's shoulders. 'Frank, I'm a married man with daughters.'

A squawk of gulls erupts along Esmonde Road, heading west. 'That'll be young Timmy Curnow out with his shanghai, I reckon!' says Frank. 'Goodbye you old bastard, goodbye little girl with the gin-drinker's voice. Oh and I do

VANYA AND BILL ANSO

hope the party goes well tonight. Can't stand parties m'self though, eh, nasty loud affairs!'

Then my Old Man retrieves his pushbike from behind the overgrown hedge and, with me Queen of the Castle on his shoulders, mounts and sets off on the long journey towards the Devonport ferry. Which leaves Frank, suddenly overcome and chuckling with a good idea for another story, to go in and scribble down a few notes before feeding a fresh green sheet of paper into his typewriter ready for the morning.

IN THE BIG ROOM

IN THE BIG Room, which used to be the Ballroom before the renovations, afternoon tea is served to my mother's relatives, using the best china. In the photo taken by Grandpop Cornes, it's Aunty Joyce and Uncle Alister McLeod and their children who are visiting. Janet is close to Robin in age and Susan to Judy, but I fall between them and the youngest two, Ian and Mary, so I'm not really close to any of them. Besides,they live down south in Napier so we hardly ever see them.

Here we all are on Saturday afternoon with Gran Cornes on the left. This is our thin Gran, who will take us kids into her gracious Herne Bay mansion the times when my mother is away, or in hospital for that operation to fix her hearing. Or when our new baby sister is born. Or again later when my mother needs a hysterectomy for a fibrous growth the size of an orange, symptoms of which Dr M had dismissed as 'just the change'. Gran, though of strict Victorian upbringing, is not really such a Tartar as some people imagine. She always phones before my birthday and asks me if I, 'the bookworm of the family', want the latest Enid Blyton for my present. (I *do*!) The Cornes' garden is good to play in, mainly because we're allowed to pick as much as we like of the feijoa and red guava fruit. Pink-flowering balsam shrubs grow along the driveway with their funny green seed pods you can pop so they turn into caterpillars. And out front there's holly that the kids in the orphanage over the road come and steal every Christmas at the risk of getting told off by Gran.

Once when we're staying there, we go up Clifton Road to wait for the tram to school, but a man tells us there'll be no school today, it's a holiday, kiddies —

ABOVE: Gran, McLeods, Rene & Tilly Percy visiting.
BELOW: Joyce & Alister on our 'stage'

Pop & Gran;
9 Clifton Road

don't we know that the *King* is dead? When we run back and tell Gran, she lets us look through her scrapbooks of the two happy princesses and their playhouse and the corgis, and now shy Lizzie is going to be Queen, how about that, girls?

And it is Gran and Grandpop who generously pay out for my frightful orthodontic braces, which are meant to stop me looking like a bulldog. Once, when these have been removed to my brown paper lunch-bag so I can chew my lunch, they get absentmindedly thrown into the school incinerator and all the caretaker finds are some squiggly bits of wire. It's Gran and Grandpop who fork out for replacement braces, and it's they who buy the Lowrys their first and only fridge in the early 1950s, a sturdy little Leonard (which, touch wood, is still going strong in my bach fifty years later). And when Grandpop grows too frail with Parkinson's disease to drive, my mother and father are lucky enough to inherit the Cornes' grey Hillman Minx and, aged forty, learn to drive their first car (which will come to a sad end near the Albany pub, but that's another story . . .).

The lady here with Cousin Mary reading on her knee is Gran's sister Rene, like Gran a competent artist. Her paintings are still treasured, like the lovely study of apples and foliage above my desk as I write, or those wild roses on the safe door in the red bach at the shared family property by the Wade River. But my mother hated being named for her aunt 'Reenee' and always insisted on being called 'Ireen'. Poor Great-Aunty Rene would end her days in a nursing home suffering from dementia, recognising no one. Next to her sits our great-grandmother, the widow Tilly Percy, who would live to ripe old age in her nineties. When each of us had to give her a kiss, her cheek was as dry and soft as old chamois leather. She would then give us each a lovely ten-shilling note to buy all our Christmas presents for the family. (After she died, there was only Great-Aunty Hester (Hetty) standing between Gran and the money from the sale of Ellison Chambers on Queen Street. I remember as a gauche teenager coming home from school to

Ellison Chambers on Queen Street

be told of the death of dear old Hetty. How it shames me that I jumped up and down in glee, shouting, 'Now we'll be rich, we'll be rich!', much to Mummy's astonishment and horror. And since Gran Cornes lived to be 101, it would be a long time before any of the Ellison Chambers money trickled down to my generation, and then only because my mother died before Gran.)

Look at those lovely great picture-windows in the Big Room, and isn't that a London Underground poster pinned to the wall? And there on the floor by Irene's knees sit I, at that time still her pet with that sunny smile (and probably grubby feet). Cousin Janet is standing at the back, wearing a dress in her family tartan. Next to her, Robin is wearing that red dress with the little white spots, one of the few of hers that I actually looked forward to growing into. Judy is behind me in grey, looking pretty as usual, and Cousin Susan next to her.

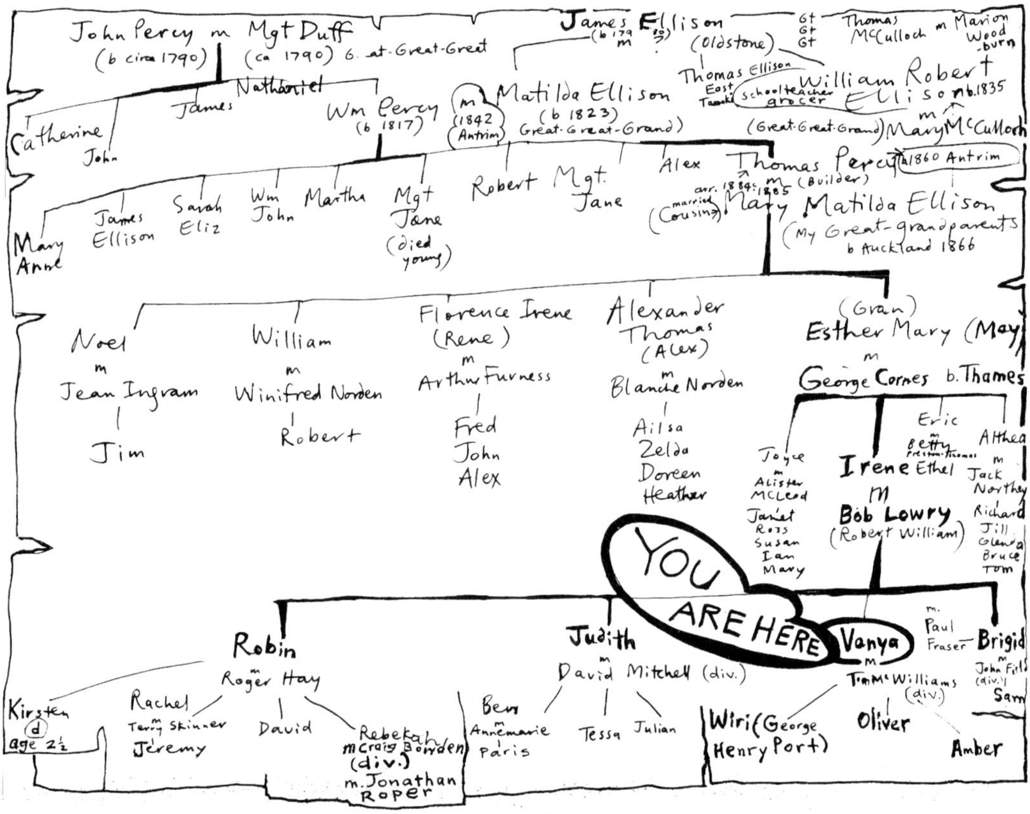

SOMETIMES WHEN POP visits with Gran, they bring their other daughter, Aunty Althea, with our slightly younger cousins Jill and Richard Northey. These are even happier occasions. The grown-ups sit round in the big armchairs and, while they talk, sip tea and read out letters from Aunty Joyce, we kids hit the dress-up box and maybe make up a play or concert. With the heavy curtain drawn across the three steps at one end, we have our stage. And when everything is ready I will draw back the curtain with a flourish of pretend trumpets and shoosh the unruly grown-ups. If reluctant to settle down, they will be bribed with glasses of dry sherry, or citrus wine with the nifty name, Lemora.

Cousin Richard, who's said to have a genius IQ above 150, can recite the whole of 'The mountain sheep are sweeter/But the village sheep are fatter,/We therefore deemed it meeter/To carry off the latter . . .'. Not surprisingly, he will grow up to be both city councillor and a Labour MP. Robin loves showing off on the piano with her 'Chopsticks' and 'Für Elise', and Judy will do a dance from her Nettleton-Edwards class. In the Shakespeare skits (written by me), Richard, being the only boy, gets to play the handsome Prince, while blonde Jill (who will become an optometrist) plays Princess. Robin and Judy will be roped in as Wicked King and Stepmother, while I of course will take the plum role of Witch. 'Bubble bubble, toil and trouble, there are no cobwebs among *this* rubble . . . Ah ha HAARRR!'

This sunny afternoon room where we kids love to put on entertainments is very different from the room it will be when the rellies have left. As evening ripens bohemian guests will start arriving. By the time the roistering poet Jim returns with my father, bearing goodies for the feast, there will be George-and-Pauline-Fraser, Noeline-and-Bob-Chapman, Bob-and-Cath-Tizard already sipping the wine they've brought. Poet Rex Fairburn arrives, banging his head on the top of the kitchen doorway as usual, and bringing a strange bottle with different coloured liqueurs in four compartments, with neat crystal stoppers. We kids take it into the hall to sample, but my sisters, the big mingies, only grudgingly let me have any. I get a few glugs of something called cherry brandy and it is sweet and potent, not like the yucky homebrew or sour burgundy our parents sometimes let us have a taste of. It makes me feel all giggly, different, happy. So when my mother asks me to clean out the smelly cage of our budgie, Harry Lime, right away, I cheerfully replace his poopy newspaper carpet, give him a new piece of dry cuttlefish to sharpen his little beak on, plus fresh water and his greens of puha from the garden. And it has never seemed so much fun before.

It's early so my father is mellow. He tells me it's time for the music, so off I go to turn on the gramophone. Selecting a party record, I carefully place the needle in the groove and away it goes, music from the 'Royal Fireworks Suite', maybe, or some other light classical stuff to start with. Dreamily I will sashay around the empty room till the party spills over from the kitchen as more guests arrive. Some jealous husband, thinking a tall blue-black Negro is flirting with his wife, will crossly haul her off home early. And later we will hear about the blonde secretary who brought the Negro along: she will get visited by the cops but will toss her deal-bag of the 'evil weed' marijuana into the washing-machine while it's going, and those drongos will never think of looking there. What a hoot!

My uncle has brought Kumeu plonk decanted into a chianti bottle, which he will take home when empty at the end of the evening. A grumpy-looking neighbour comes over to ask us to keep the music down a bit this time, please. The guests gradually become merrier and louder and greatly enjoy themselves prancing about the well-polished floor doing variations on the Brontosaurus Stomp, a dance of my father's own invention. Gradually, as the grog goes down, they will progress from awfully sober to happy to merry to all the funny words I looked up in the dictionary and thesaurus for *drunk*, like flushed, befuddled, fonged, tiddly, tipsy, tight, half-cut, obfuscated, squiffy, soaked, sozzled, screwed, shickered, spifflicated, stoked, primed, pissed, mellow, maudlin, muzzy, bosky, boozed, bibacious, bibulous, inebriated, intoxicated, debauched, dissipated, wild, half seas over and three sheets to the wind....

And oh, the dancing, the dancing! All the while I will be shyly hiding away in the dark corner by the gramophone changing the dance records. My father will be grand in his zoot suit, with his best shirt (ironed by me), a tie (handknitted by my mother), his black hair slicked back, his favourite brothel-creepers on his feet. Once, at the end of his usual long busy day, he had pulled those shoes off and out crawled a very tired and squashed weta. He said he'd felt a vague lump all day but not bothered to investigate. I must say that's the only time I ever felt sorry for a weta!

My mother will be dancing a bit more sedately, whirling around gracefully, barefoot, in peasant blouse and circular gypsy skirt. The kauri floor will be

The Brontosaurus Stomp

ABBREVIATED BILL OF FOODSTUFFS

Whores d'œuvres & Canopies

Cold Tongue Sandwiches Hunky Dory. Devilled Parsons' Noses. Spermicelli in Aspic. Doe Nuts. Jellied Ova. Stripped Cheesecake. Petits Matelots. Hard Tack. Gallstones. Cabin Dog Biscuits. Ambergris. Pigs' Bladders. Slugs. Ratnip. Frogs' Trotters.

Soups

Scotch Brothel. Union Consomme. Mess of Potage. Eau de Cabbagio.

Fishes

Holy Mackerel. Bit of a Cod. Electric Eel Bob Semple. Stuffed Sea Urchin. Silverfish. Soused Gourmet. Fish Rarssoles. Cat & Dog Fish. Smoked Lamprey. Raspberry Jellyfish. Crawfish Politico. Cheap Skate. Sordines. Crabs.

Fowls

Swallowtails. Roast Buzzard. Gulls' Blizzards. Braised Pigeons' Breasts Berlei. Cuckoo. Stewed Vulture. Stuffed Birds au Rakehelly. Screwed Chickens. Spanish Fly. Stool Pigeon. Fanny Tails. Pea Cocks. Shags. Tits.

Cold Carcase Meats (no coupons needed)

Mutton Birds. Bulging Sausage. Cold Shoulder & Knuckles (*see Forcemeats*). Dogs' Trotters. Bloody Pudding. Meat Abstract. Potted Guts. Cold Eunuchorn. Caxton Press Rump. Cold Cows' Breasts (*Go Easy—Think of Udders*)

Hot Flesh

Lion Chops. Black Sausage. Hind Quarto Elephant. Roast Ox Buttock au John Pull. Angels on Horesback. Saddle of Venuson. Lambkins. Belly of Pork. Taradiddle. Horseflesh Anglais. Gooseflesh Americain. Boiled Tripe. Stewed Stag. Fatted Calves. Hocks. Horse's Neck. Hot Dags.

Stuffings & Forcemeats

Jammed Tarts. Ground Mays. Stuck Pig. Stuffed Goat (with Relish). Bulgarian Bugs. Cold Shag. Jerked Hare With Gherkins. Chocolate Blocks. Toed In The Hole. Banana Splits. Angelica Strips. Festoonēd Lentils. Pulled Pudding. Hump au Chameau. Stuffed Ox Tail. Raw Muscles.

PIECE DE RESISTANCE (THIS ONE'S TOUGH!)

ye olde roaſt ſucking pig caxton

Salauds (without dressing!)

French Lettuce. Water-caress. Turnup. Four-leaf Glover. Spring Unions. Dandy Lie-in. Maidenhair. Cocksfoot. Bungers. Shoots.

Vegies

Leeks. Peas. Artyblokes. Toads Tools. Cauliflower Glovear. Shuffler O'Grattan. Chips That Pass In The Night. Dried Apricots. Nuts. Dates. Roots.

Sweeties

Monkey Nuts Cassees. Stuffed Olive. Rolypoly & Hot Bed Rolls. Trifles. Bikelets. Queen Podding. Hominy. Chafed Dates. Lady's Fingers. Moosemeal. Apricocks. Tarts. Dumpings. Twists & Rolls (with Cocoa Butter). American Boss.

China Dishes

Ground Lice. Fish Balls. Plover's & Curnow's Eggs. Flitters. Gobbet Soup. Plonk. Snails' Horn. Aunts' Eggs. Hips & Haws. Sinkist Navels.

Dainties for Diabetics (prescription required)

Spewed Prunes. Nutty Joy. Sugar Candies. Turkish Delight. Stickjaws. Eskimo Pie. Waffles (with Mulattoes, Treacle or Mabel Stirrup). Chocolate Creams. Changing Balls. Black Balls. Nougat. Toffee Apples. Allenbury's Risks.

Topoffs & Unsavouries

Gentle Cheeses (mild). Cheeseparings. Mixed Nuts. Buttered Crumpet. Big Heels. Button Hooks. Shoe Horns. Jams. Cigars. Mineral Waters. Stomach Bumps. Tooth Picks (Take Your Pick!)

heaving with my big sisters in flirting dances with their prospective boyfriends and all the gyrating 'poets, lovers and the houseless poor' immortalised in that poem Jim Baxter wrote called 'Auckland'.

But my mother would later write a poem too, remembering the dancing, after the suicide of her friend Liz Rotherham.

Elizabeth
You were one of two
young girls who danced at parties
to Bach barefooted.
The kitchen packed with bodies
floated loud
with beer-warmed conversation and with roaring clash of egos.
But your feet
bare on the brown boards
of the lower room
patterned an oasis by the gramophone.
And I can see you still
your face absorbed
in rhythm with old scratched seventy-eights,
your careful feet
compelled by gigue and rondo and badinerie.

Everyone will be having *such* a good time it will be hard getting guests to leave. But, sent off to bed before midnight, I will be overexcited and unable to sleep because of the noises of music and loud laughter, the occasional crash of glass or someone shouting, 'Faark the bloody neighbours!', and because some sozzled poet or artist might try getting into bed with me by mistake. At some stage, maybe around dawn, my father will come out onto the stage with a loud-hailer booming, 'This is the voice of Doom. *Go home*!' Meanwhile, throughout the early hours of the morning, guests may be heard in the spare cubicle huffing and gasping and giggling and shooshing each other, and if I wake I might get up to watch them going at it. Only afterwards, as they share a smoke or swig from a wine jar, will they notice my solemn little sleepy head over the cubicle wall and tell me to 'Fark off and stop playing the bloody gooseberry!'

Cheese
Spread
CHEESE

Mayonnaise

WHEN MORNING COMES, we kids are the first ones up, eager to discover any lipsticks, hankies, coins or other treasure carelessly dropped in the course of the evening, maybe a pack with a couple of fags still in it (to share with the Bullyboys) or a bottle stashed away and forgotten and miraculously still unopened. Often a few leftover guests will be still snoring, curled up in ones and twos on sofas and spare beds.

Now I've poured all the stinky dregs from bottles and sticky glasses into the big brown coffee-pot. When my father comes out, he has such a hangover that he boils this witch's brew up in a saucepan and drinks half a cup before realising it isn't coffee. Giggling, we kids begin attacking the mess, washing all the glasses, supper plates, cooking pots and pans. We empty the overflowing scallop-shell ashtrays, stack beer bottles, wrap up broken glass in newspaper for the rubbish, and mop the floor where drinks were spilt.

Tousled old Jim comes barefoot up to the kitchen, purple-mouthed and hugging an empty wine-jar he has slept the night with. Cracking six raw eggs into a bowl he pours them down his throat, then some beer and then, sitting at my mother's old typewriter, proceeds to write a beautiful love poem. Whatever happened to that poem, I wonder?

Down in the Big Room the smells of stale beer and smoke have seeped into the armchair coverings (of checked shirt material given by Sam Leathem from his Summit shirt factory), so we throw the French doors wide. As it's early summer, at least there are no ashes in the fireplace to clean out. The fireplace is between the stage and the radiogram, and is built of bricks handmade by Grandpa Lowry when he was rebuilding the house. Several of them have little pawprints where Ponsonby and his faithful Remuera stepped in the damp clay while the bricks were lying in the sun to set. Over summer the fireplace lies empty, or filled with one of Robin's artistic dried arrangements, while the armchairs are facing out to the patio in a semicircle with the wistaria bush beyond.

It's here my mother likes to sit with a fag and cup of tea in the stretch of lazy late afternoon, hoping for some peace and listening to her favourite records, mostly string concertos by Brahms, Beethoven, Bach, Schubert, Schumann, Mozart. I lean over her shoulder. 'Mummy, what's "the bloody gooseberry"?'

But in winter the chairs are arranged around the hearth, and it's one of my chores to clean out last night's ashes from the grate, chuck them out under the

FROM: The Sky is a Limpet:

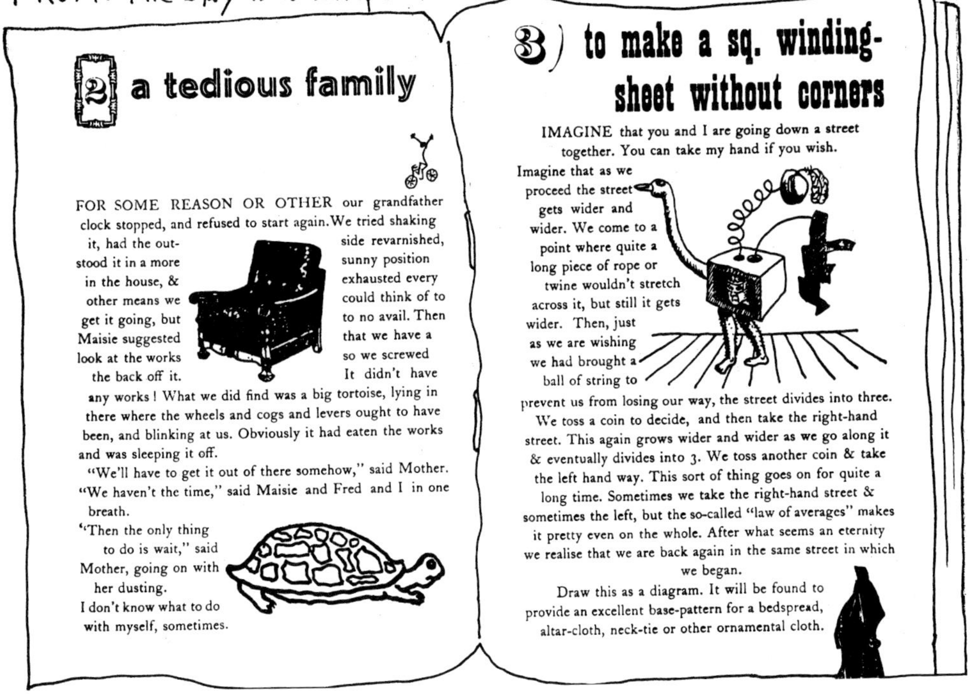

2 a tedious family

FOR SOME REASON OR OTHER our grandfather clock stopped, and refused to start again. We tried shaking it, had the outside revarnished, stood it in a more sunny position in the house, & exhausted every other means we could think of to get it going, but to no avail. Then Maisie suggested that we have a look at the works so we screwed the back off it. It didn't have any works! What we did find was a big tortoise, lying in there where the wheels and cogs and levers ought to have been, and blinking at us. Obviously it had eaten the works and was sleeping it off.

"We'll have to get it out of there somehow," said Mother.

"We haven't the time," said Maisie and Fred and I in one breath.

"Then the only thing to do is wait," said Mother, going on with her dusting.

I don't know what to do with myself, sometimes.

3) to make a sq. winding-sheet without corners

IMAGINE that you and I are going down a street together. You can take my hand if you wish.

Imagine that as we proceed the street gets wider and wider. We come to a point where quite a long piece of rope or twine wouldn't stretch across it, but still it gets wider. Then, just as we are wishing we had brought a ball of string to prevent us from losing our way, the street divides into three. We toss a coin to decide, and then take the right-hand street. This again grows wider and wider as we go along it & eventually divides into 3. We toss another coin & take the left hand way. This sort of thing goes on for quite a long time. Sometimes we take the right-hand street & sometimes the left, but the so-called "law of averages" makes it pretty even on the whole. After what seems an eternity we realise that we are back again in the same street in which we began.

Draw this as a diagram. It will be found to provide an excellent base-pattern for a bedspread, altar-cloth, neck-tie or other ornamental cloth.

citrus trees, and get the fire going. It's quite easy. You twist up some newspaper and a little tepee of kindling, but if the kindling is damp you hold a sheet of newspaper across the whole fireplace to encourage the flame to take till it becomes a nice blaze. Then you can add chunky logs and black coke that will pop and splutter, making spark 'soldiers' in the chimney. Each of us kids will choose a particular spark and the one whose soldier 'dies' last is the winner.

On winter Sunday nights my mother will make her *terribly* nourishing vegetable soup with hot buttered scones, plain or cheese-flavoured. My father will be there in his corner armchair and we will all sit around the fire like a real family, talking about . . . oh, about things like their magazine *Here & Now* (fondly known by subscribers as 'Now & Then'), or our school reports (oo-er!) or maybe Robin's latest successful artwork. But sometimes things turn sour when my father starts going on about our big sis going down the graveyard with *that boy* again, and I will eat quickly and creep away to my room before the shouting starts.

One night, when something had gone awfully wrong for him at work, my father came home late from the pub to find his dinner all dried out on top of the stove and the pot ruined. On top of his bad bad day this was the last straw, and he started shouting and raging at every little thing. When I crept up to the kitchen he was snarling and cursing and dragging my mother around the kitchen floor by a hank of her hair.

Before thinking, I grabbed the carving knife from the drawer and plunged it towards him, growling, 'Stop that, Daddy, or I swear I will kill you!' Amazingly, he did stop, and he and my mother were both flushed and embarrassed, telling me it was nothing, just a little argument ....

Another time he didn't like the way I sat at the table near him, chewing celery loudly with my mouth open, and he suddenly swiped me across the head so hard I fell off my chair. As I picked myself up to run away to my room, I heard my mother ask him, 'Was that really necessary, Bob?' And he just grabbed the bowl of pink junket sprinkled with nutmeg that was for dessert (his favourite!) and flung it at the ceiling, roaring, 'FAAARK THE JUNKET!'

His sober excuse next morning may have been that he'd been drowning his sorrows because his press was going under, but still I made sure I never sat within hitting distance of him again.

Bob with Venus under the plum-tree

NOW, THOUGH, ON this Sunday morning I've run to sit in my usual possie on my mother's knees for a cuddle against her soft-curving belly. But today she straight away slides me off, suggesting I grind some coffee. So I do, in the old coffee-grinder my father dug up from the garden once. When the coffee is brewed and stirred, left to settle then stirred again, and I've poured out cups for all the grown-ups, strong and black and heady-smelling, I curl up under the table among the assorted legs. I'm hoping the grown-ups will forget I'm there, so I can peek up the trouser leg of the 'wild colonial boy', an author called Maurice. I've been told by my sisters that he has an artificial leg and I want to know if it's true, and it is. Quiet as a mouse I wait, hoping they're going to discuss the fascinating topic of babies and where they come from, which I'm not absolutely sure about yet. One of the Bullyboys did try and show me once, secretly down the olive-grove. But can it be just that, the bloke lying on the lady and sticking his diddle into her crack and peeing, can it, with all that panting an' huffing an' groaning an' shooshing an' carrying *on*? Making *babies*?

But now I nearly drowse off, curled in a comfy little ball in the kitchen this fine morning as the sun through plum-tree leaves dapples and warms the room. From my hidey-hole I can hear the birds singing in the plum tree, the sour orange, the monkey-apple beside the hole in the hedge through to Jammy and Jojo's house. And I can pretend my Daddy isn't really a drunken sot, but a proud man who will love it when my mother presents him with a fine son, a son to be called Robert William the Third perhaps, at last a son to help him in his vegetable garden and tend his compost heap and be his good apprentice in the printery, the way we girls were never expected to.

Yes, this Sunday morning things must be going as well at the press as they are at home, deadlines must have been met and bills paid, for my father seems in such a good mood, and he and Jim are raving on. But then my mother remembers I'm under the table and gently tells me to run outside and play. She says they have some grown-up matter to discuss, which I expect may have something to do with one of the tipsy poets borrowing a headmaster's wife last night, which I pretend to know nothing about. Anyway, I drift away while they discuss this problematical state of affairs, 'not for little girls' ears'.

After noticing Harry Lime still needs some bird seed, I get it for him, then take his budgie cage out in the garden and try teaching him to say 'Pretty

LEFT: Robin in brown velvet.
ABOVE: Robin, Judy, Vanya (in brown velvet!)

Polly', without success. I wander through the hole in the overgrown hedge to look for Jojo or Jammy. But they aren't in the playhouse, or on the tennis court playing against their big sisters and brother or the Maidments from down Fern Avenue. In the end Jojo's giggling gives him away — he's up the monkey-apple tree. So I climb up after him and join him throwing monkey-apples down on anyone going past, and other monkey games for a while. Then I get this great idea. At least it seems like a great idea to me.

'Let's run away, Jojo. Have you got any pocket money left? I can get a loaf of bread, some cheese and apples, and we could catch a tram down to the highway then hitch rides south. . . .'

He's got a whole shilling in his pocket, but adds 'Nah, Vanna, Mater said I'm not to do anything silly with you, remember what happened last time?' We'd sampled some tender carrots from Eady's garden, for 'waste not want not' is what I say. Then we'd wandered down the Park and hidden in somebody's strange wild garden, where Jojo had idly torn bits of green juicy-looking leaf off a big plant and chewed them up. Then we'd played on the lullaby, one each end, swinging higher and higher till Jojo complained of feeling sick. So then we'd hidden inside the roundabout, squeezing through a small gap in the broken part, sitting on the spokes as it turned creakily round and round. And maybe we'd never have been found if Jojo hadn't got that crook tummy. When night was coming, we heard his Mater calling him and he scrambled out and ran to her, crying and vomiting. When she heard that he'd eaten only a bit of crusty bread, a few bites of apple . . . oh, and a leaf off that plant over there, she got really wild. It was just as well Jojo's father, the doctor, had had experience of poisonous tropical plants during his war in New Caledonia, where he'd been a colonel, because he was able to identify the plant and pump out the stuff in Jojo's tummy, and save his life. But after that I was 'a bad influence, a very bad influence'.

'Well, we could go and play in the wheat bin?' (How I loved the cool silky feel of rivers of wheat grains against my bare brown legs.) 'No? Well, maybe we could pick some of your mum's flowers and set up a stall in the Park then?' But he reminds me that, although last time we had managed to sell several bunches of the Mater's prize roses with baby-breath and maidenhair fern, she got so ropable she made us give the money away to charity. So that's out too. In the end we just climb up to the reservoir to throw sheep dung into the town water supply.

On the way home we climb the best tree and take turns pushing each other on our favourite bouncing branch. There are no Bad Men about, thank goodness. Once an ugly old Bad Man wearing a suit and hat had offered Jojo lollies. And when Jojo accepted a couple, the Bad Man grabbed hold of him and dragged him into his black car that looked like a monster beetle. Knowing I'd be in for trouble if Jojo was driven away, I had to get into the car too. And then the Bad Man pulled me onto his knee and let me steer the car along Puriri Drive, but he was poking his finger up my crack and he was wiggling it around harder and harder and I didn't like it but I got scared and didn't know what to do. Then, driving past our place, I was pleased to see Daddy working in the garden. So I called out and waved to him but he didn't hear, and the Bad Man said some really *wicked* swear-words, and stopped around the corner to let me and Jojo out. He said he would come back and kill me if I ever told anyone about him. So I never did.

But my sisters greet me now with the news that Harry Lime's escaped over the hedge. We will never see him again.

WE BONNY LOWRY girls really loved our food, eh! My mother, though not keen on housework, used to cook good dinners considering we were as poor as the proverbial church mice, as she often said. We always knew which day of the week it was by what she cooked. Fridays, fish or sausage and mash, with 'cabbagio' or cauli or silverbeet from my father's garden.

If there was no party happening on Saturdays, there'd be roast mutton or beef with thick gravy, and spuds of course, and green veg, and yellows like carrot or pumpkin or kumara. Or those horrid watery chokos from the vine (donated by Rex Fairburn) that was going berserk and taking over the plum tree. And I loathed the wild Jerusalem artichokes because they tasted like dead ants and made me gag, so my mother said I didn't have to eat them. Sunday would be the veg soup and scones. Monday it would be cottage pie, or rice with leftover cubes of roast curried with plump juicy raisins. It was to me Mummy gave the wooden skewers from the roast with chunks of meat still on them, because I was the youngest and her pet — but not for long! Tuesday it was the disgustingly 'good-for-you-liver-once-a-week' with fried bacon. On

Butterscotch pudding

½ cup br. sugar + 1 tbsp butter in saucepan – stir till sugar dissolved. Pour into greased dish, place apricot halves (drained) on top (cut side up)

Sift 6 ozs flour + pinch salt, make well, stir in 2 beaten eggs, add gradually ¾ pint milk – beat constantly till like thick cream. Stand in cold place. Pour into mold cover w. gr. proof paper + steam 1 hr. Serve w. apricot sauce.

Wednesday-before-payday, tripe 'at only fourpence a pound!' with onions in white sauce, or maybe macaroni cheese. On Thursday, Irish stew, with tinned peas for a treat.

Sometimes there was pudding after, apple sponge with top milk, or rhubarb crumble or butterscotch pudding or fudge pudding or marmalade steamed pudding or vanilla rice pudding with raisins, when I liked to quote, 'What *is* the matter with Mary Jane? ... *it's lovely rice pudding for dinner again*!' from A. A. Milne. Once, in a good mood, Mummy told us about the time she'd been staying at her cousin Zelda's and there was rice pudding with raisins. She'd carefully put the raisins aside around the rim of the plate, her special treat to eat at the end, but Zelda's mother, thinking young Irene disliked raisins, went and took her plate and the delicious raisins away, so you should never save the best bits till last, eh?

After a glass of plonk my mother taught us lots of sensible things to remember all our lives. Things like a stitch in time saves nine; all that glitters is not gold; two blacks don't make a white; people in glasshouses shouldn't throw stones; a bird in the hand is worth two in the bush; you can't make a silk purse out of a sow's ear; a burnt child fears the fire; all cats look alike in the dark; make hay while the sun shines; and gather ye rosebuds while ye may.

Meanwhile, my father would go for his grog to the nearest pub after work, maybe down the Queen's Ferry with his mates, other printers, or maybe artists or writers or a journalist like his mate Dave. He and Dave might turn up at Dave's house late and so greatly fonged that Dave's wife would hurl Dave's dried-out spaghetti bolognaise at him, telling him and his drunken friend to bugger off and what's more not to bother coming home till he'd sobered up. So my father would bring Dave home to share his own dinner, which was good because while Dave was there my father would be merry. I liked Dave.

When our birthdays came around, my mother would bake a special cake. It was the only time she made cakes. She'd ask us what sort of cake we'd like. Mine was always the pretty marble cake, all cochineal pink, vanilla yellow and chocolate, with sometimes white butter-icing and rainbow hundreds-and-thousands or silver cachous on it if you were lucky. And the other treat every birthday was, she'd take us kids on the tram to the Golden Dragon Cafe at the foot of Greys Avenue, where we'd order our chicken chop sueys, or chow meins with crispy noodles. You could go out the back, through the frantic

Old Maharajah

nut brown ale

A connoisseur vintage ale of rare bouquet, high calorific content and admirable nutritive properties, rich in vitamins and literary associations, and especially blended for those who value the finer things of life and to whom hops and malt are something more than mere matters of commerce.

BOTTLED BY DOBBIE, FRASER, LOWRY, MUNRO INC.

Taste its Tangy Goodness

steamy kitchen to the loo, where there was a crate of colourful apple-wrapping paper to wipe yourself on. Then you'd go back to your pew to eat as much as you could of the stack of 'unhealthy!' white buttered bread while waiting for Daddy to roll in (usually late after stopping at a pub on his way from the press). That wasn't so bad, for usually he wasn't the cafe's only slightly sozzled customer. But after the cheap meal, if he and my mother hadn't had some argument over him being late and were still on speaking terms, and could afford it, we'd all proceed to the Civic to see some good wholesome family movie. My father could be counted on to embarrass us, for, being late, all of us would have to stumble past a row of knees. Then he'd yell out things like, 'Stop mumbling, goddammit, man!' to Marlon Brando. Then he'd have to stumble out again, swearing, past grumpy knees to go for a leak.

AFTER THE BIG TIDY-UP

AFTER THE BIG tidy-up this Sunday arvo, when all the visitors have sloped off, my father comes out of the French doors of his study to take a leak in the sage bush. He looks all embarrassed noticing me on the path by the back door, where I'm crouching by my upside-down bike, mixing up some apricot paint with some white paint I found out in the shed.

'What are you doing, Pudding?'

After muttering that at nine I'm too old to be called baby names, I tell him I'm going to paint my half-size bike a nice pale apricot, to decorate with rainbow crepe papers and enter in the Best Decorated Bike competition at the school fair next Saturday. But he just shakes his head and goes inside, tut-tutting. Then, as I'm wondering why the paint is a vulgar baby-pink and not quite the lovely pale apricot I'd hoped for, he comes out again saying, 'But listen, Pudding, next Saturday we've got free tickets to *The Sleeping Prince* as I'm printing their programmes. Wouldn't you rather come to that with me?'

Stubbornly starting to paint my little bike, I shake my head, informing my father that *The Sleeping Prince* sounds like some sissy ballet that our dainty ballerina of the family, Judy, would probably prefer.

So on the following Saturday I will get caught in heavy rain on my way to the school fair, causing the carefully entwined crepe paper to totally disintegrate, and then to top it off my bright pink bike will get a puncture and I will have to walk all the way home, catching a 'streamig cod-id-the-node'. And how I will wish I had taken up my father's offer instead, especially when Judy tells me excitedly afterwards that it wasn't a soppy ballet at all but a terrific play starring the great British actress Sybil Thorndike and her husband Lewis Casson, and I would've *loved* it!

However, something comes of that puncture later. I leave the bike at the Greenwoods Corner bike shop, having the puncture fixed. When I go in to pick it up, the Bike Man will say, 'Oh, yes, your mother said you're to choose from one of these bikes', pointing to the brand-new ladies' bikes all in such a gleaming row it would take your breath away.

'Oh no, no, I've just come to get my little pink bike, this one with the puncture, you know.'

'No, little girl, I'm sure your mother wanted you to choose one of these. Why don't you use our phone, give her a call and ask her?'

So I do, and to my amazement my mother says yes, I can choose a new ladies' bike, as I can ride it to school and save tramfares, eh? So in shocked delight I choose a lovely dark-red Humber, and ride it home. It will take my mother years to pay off, a little bit put by every week for that and for the rehab loan on our One Tree Hill property. And the little pink bike will be sent on up to Opononi to Jenny and Robert Lee-Johnson, who are younger than me and can probably use it for a while to ride around their country roads.

MY FATHER'S STUDY seems to me a very special place. One whole wall is jam-packed bookshelves, and the opposite side consists of conservatory windows recycled from the old house, which cast a greenish light and give onto the vegetable garden by the revolving clothes-line and the Park beyond. Sometimes I need to know something for a school project, but it's never wise to disturb my father in his study as he might be trying to write some difficult editorial for his magazine with deadlines upon him. He will just grunt or curse at my requests, like 'How many days would it take to drive a horse-drawn caravan around Ireland, Daddy?', mumbling that just because his father was from Donegal doesn't mean he knows all things Irish. And he will grumblingly

thrust some reference books like the *Great Reader's Digest Atlas* or the *Shorter Oxford Dictionary* at me, telling me to push off.

But now, when he's busy out in the garden turning his compost heap, I creep into the study and, on my mother's old typewriter, slowly tap out my first quirky comedy. It's about this Queen who collects lost handkerchiefs, and her stroppy daughter Prancine. And to sterilise these hankies Queenie boils them up in her big soup pot, then goes to have a lie-down. Prancine comes by, sniffs what's in the pot and gives it a good stir with the wooden spoon, then goes away. And in comes the King, who takes a good sip of it and declares, 'Hmmm, not as good as her usual soup.'

And when my play wins a prize in the British Drama League contest, I will earn two whole pounds, enough to buy my first long-playing record, a good jazzy Frank Sinatra thing, for 39s 6d, with sixpence change. Plus I will get my photo in the *Star* as 'Schoolgirl Playwright' and my father will be as proud as any father ever was. And he will take me seriously and not ask, 'What's this rubbish Pudding's writing now?' as he does when my mother, to earn fifty pounds, is typing out a manuscript about a place called Coal Flat for a friend, Bill Pearson, ready to send to the publisher, and I am helping her with some pages while teaching myself two-finger typing.

But I have always enjoyed the feeling of being useful, eh? Our mother has always been the sort of person who is extremely useful. Like she organises huge jumble sales of piles of fusty-smelling clothes, battered old shoes and squashed hats and handbags and useless 'white elephants' on trestles in the Big Room, for some China friendship or family planning charity or other. Or she might need to arrange a cot and tiny baby clothes and bottles and advice for a bewildered Dutch couple who have applied to adopt a baby and don't quite know what to do with it when they get one straight away. Or much later she will visit murderers in prison, will take me and my teenaged sister with her so the poor guys can get a look at our perky nipples through tight summer dresses and have someone to dream about and correspond with in their lonely cells.

Yes, it is good to be useful, isn't it? There are not that many things I'm able to feel useful at when I'm only nine, though. Well, I suppose helping with the dishes when it's my rostered turn. Or going down the long muddy bush track past the hollow tree where big creepy-crawlies or even evil witches might be lurking, down to the street letterbox come rain or shine to collect the morning milk, and in the evening for the mail and the *Star* to check if Peter Pan has used one of my sketches or poems or stories, contributions to the Children's Page, giving me more points towards that longed-for book voucher.

My arithmetic wasn't too good in this early story, eh?

> Babbs is 20. Baby is only 1. Mother is about 29. Father is 39. Mother is calling her children to come in to the house. After dinner they all go out for a walk. Babbs says, Mother we did not bring our coats today. Then it began to rain and they had to go home and get dry. Then Father made a fire and they all sat down and had tea. Soon it began to pour, and the rain broke the house down. When it did, it was burnt and they all had to run for their lives. Father says they should get into his car and drive away, but Mother says no that is a silly idea because they might get burnt and they had gone too far. After a time they came to a shop. Babbs says, We will work where we can. So they worked at the shop for a year and then the shop got on fire, so they ran and ran and ran until the whole world got on fire and there was not one single person to be seen on the lands and world. So the whole world was all gone.

Or, as my style (and tenses) improve, it might be some nice poem about 'Violets in a Wood' or 'Morning in Cornwall Park' or 'At the Beach':

> Little girl in a faded dress
> walking down the path,
> where is she going in the heat of the day,
> a sun-bleached curl over dark eyes?
> She scuffles bare toes in the hot white dust
> and hums a soft sweet tune,
> over the short sea grass she goes
> down the broken steps and along.
> Across the streaked sand she skips alone,
> across to the rocks at the end.
> And there by a rockpool she crouches now

watching with wide-open eyes.
Disturbed crabs scuttle under a rock,
deep green claws and mottled backs.
Velvet brown anemones wave
under the hot gaze of the sun.
Sunlight spins, gold coin in the pool,
a shrimp madly darts through the ripples.
Throw in a stone, little brown-faced girl,
and you will hit the sun.

THROUGH THE GREAT Park we wild things, tamed into schoolgirls, cycle along to school on misty moisty Monday mornings, or today in my case lag behind till the others are out of sight because I want to be really wicked and play hookey. Of course, nobody will even notice, I think. And even if they did, what's the worst that could happen? Daddy could throw me over his knee and pretend to whack my bottom in what he calls a papax, but anyway Mummy says I'm too old for papaxes now. And she'd never use corporal punishment on any child of hers as she doesn't believe in it, or capital punishment either, whatever that is. So I'll be pretty safe as long as I don't tell her any actual lies. What the eye doesn't see the heart doesn't grieve over, eh? For in the country of the blind the one-eyed man is king. . . .

The back gate of our place leads out into the Park, where every Saturday morning hordes of pink-faced joggers trot past, much to our amusement. We girls sun ourselves on the path by the back door, waving to the buses of sightseeing tourists, calling out, 'Okay, now that you've seen the sights, you can all go home!' The Park is our backyard. Today I feel like going up to the crater to write my name and my friend Jojo's, forming VANNA LOVES JOJO with chunks of scoria. I've decided to marry him one day, even though he's a rich kid and younger than me and may become a King's College toff. (What did happen to him, anyway? I've heard he's now a disc-jockey in Sydney and Jammy went and married some nuclear physicist, or was it an Orewa dentist?) But no harm in daydreaming, eh?

Above the crater tower the two pine trees and obelisk, and I always wonder why our hill isn't called 'Two Tree Hill'. After heavy rain there's sometimes enough water to swim in the crater and you're in danger of scraping your knees on the submerged rocks, but today it'd be nice and dry. I could climb a big Moreton Bay fig and maybe spy a smelly dead lamb caught in its roots, which my father would love to know about for his compost heap, but the neighbours would *not*. Sometimes, hiding up in trees, we will throw dried lumps of sheep dung at lovers writhing under tartan rugs. On windy days we will sail our homemade kites. Wearing our oldest shorts, we will slide down muddy gullies on the sledge Pop Cornes made me, its runners greased with dripping. When that falls apart after one crash-landing too many, we'll use the big nikau palm leaves instead. Sometimes we will go exploring through the scoria caves that honeycomb under these sloping paddocks where steers and sheep safely graze. But we never do find the big tunnel Jammy told me about, the one that's supposed to run under the mountain all the way from the Waitemata to the Manukau Harbour.

The winding road leads past the Scout den where I attend Wednesday night gym-classes, which 'keeps me out of mischief', leads past the oaks and poplars and wild olives, past the Tea Kiosk and Sir John Logan Campbell's original Acacia Cottage, past the Floral Roundabout, the perfect romantic spot for weddings to be photographed, along Puriri Drive to Manukau Road. Once Robin won a prize for her painting of herself whizzing through the park on a misty moisty morning like this one. Whatever happened to that beautiful work? And whatever happened to her early promise?

Near one end of pleasantly tree-lined The Drive, Epsom, behind old stone walls and puriri trees, lurks the Normal School, where this particular Monday I will be terribly late through dreaming and dawdling. Our 'normal' motto, neatly inscribed above the front door of the great brick building, is *Success Crowns Effort*. Inside the main door there's a short flight of stairs, and the first room on the left is Miss Solomon's, where I should be sitting looking very 'normal'.

Miss Solomon is a gracious lady believed to be the sister of Queen Salote of Tonga, and her voice will be rolling mellifluously on, explaining long division, or reading some lovely long poem like Hiawatha, or getting the class to put on a play from the *School Journal* (once I'm chosen for the role of Pocahontas!). But *now* I'm too scared to go in and explain why I'm late. I can't face those rows of staring faces, I can't outstare the whole class *and* the teacher without once blinking my eyes. I can't do it, I *won't*. So I turn around and run down the stairs hell for leather, creeping off so nobody will see. Near home I crawl into one of the hollows that used to be a Maori food-pit and there I start crying because I'm a coward and don't know how to explain my colossal shyness . . . my fear of other kids laughing at me . . . pointing at my jumble-sale hand-me-down clothes . . . calling me names (though my mother has taught me that sticks and stones may break my bones but names will never hurt me) . . . and in that safe and sunny hollow feel my sad eyes of Maltexo brown closing, so I let myself go drifting off to sleep for a while. . . .

When in the golden early afternoon I wake up, I go slowly home and say, 'Teacher sent me home 'cos I's feeling sick . . .'. My mother is very kind. She gets me aspirin, a honey drink and a hottie, so I crawl under the bedclothes.

And when she tucks me in and kisses my forehead I feel terrible all right. But when Robin and Judy come riding home my mother is suddenly there at the foot of the bed, not sounding too pleased. I hide my head under the pillow so as not to meet her eyes.

'What the hell have you been up to, little madam? No answer, eh! Judy says she saw your teacher on the way home, who asked where you were today, and she had to say you must've been sick and stayed home. So where were you all day and what the bloody hell d'you think you were doing there, hmmm? Answer me!'

But what is there to say? And for the first and only time in my life, my mother gives me a good spanking.

Afterwards, lying face down on my bed, sobbing from the pain and humiliation, I decide playing hookey isn't worth the hassle. And from then on at school I will mostly try to be a model pupil, never even late for assembly. I won't play my Unblinking Staring Game any more. My exam marks will start to pick up (apart from arithmetic, of course!). I will be made a Milk Monitor! And my next teacher, Miss Hawkins, will be even more motherly, and as kindly as the Queen Mother. She will make me a Staffroom Tea Monitor, and Captain of Horete (Blue) team in basketball. Sometimes I will call her 'Mummy' by mistake, and sometimes at home will call my mother 'Miss Hawkins'. On my report Miss Hawkins will be encouraging, noting that I 'will go far in Written Expression' and that when she is an old lady in a bath-chair she will expect to see my first book published. . . .

PART TWO: BEGINNINGS

Bobby, aged 2 & 5

BELOW with Alec, Jessie & Adeline

BOBBY LOVED PARTIES

BOBBY LOVED PARTIES. Even as a devilishly handsome little boy, my father Bobby's parties were always bigger and better than anyone else's, taking up the whole of the paddock in front of the Lowry homestead Lauriston in the Hikutaia Valley on the edge of the Hauraki Plains.

Born to the sound of Paeroa church-bells, Bobby was destined to become Pope, surely, thought his exhausted mother, Jessie. I think her babe had other ideas; when the holy water was sprinkled on Bobby later, it quite definitely sizzled. But from his earliest years, even before beginning school, he was his mother's darling. One day while sewing, she noticed he was sorting out the contents of her Singer sewing-machine drawers into neat little piles, as he would soon be doing with his type fonts.

His brightness was all. Jessie could send the three-year-old to the store with a shopping-list and money and back he'd toddle sturdily with the right groceries and the right change. And he loved junket. Bobby loved junket so much he would go off to the cowshed and ask his father, Bob, for some milk for Mother to make junket, then he'd bring the milk to the kitchen, telling his mother that Father had sent some milk for her to make junket!

His mother, my grandmother, was born Janet Craig Forrest in Auckland's Ponsonby on 6 April 1887. She proudly told me, towards the end of her life, how she was descended from the architect Craig who was responsible for many of the buildings in modern Edinburgh (the Scots traditionally handed down the mother's maiden name as the middle name). Her father, William, a civil engineer from Scotland, was a drainage contractor who built all the drains in Remuera in the early 1900s. Her mother, née Janet Gibson, cared for the children: Jessie's older brother and sister, Tom and Susan, and her younger brother and sister, Bill and Grace. Jessie attended Napier Street and Ponsonby primary schools, but childhood illness meant she missed some schooling.

The family shifted to Paeroa when she was nine. She didn't much like school so, leaving at sixteen, she went dressmaking, waitressing in boarding houses and worked in a shop, then went to Wellington for eighteen months as a lady's companion. The proposal from Robert William Lowry was her fourth or fifth. Introduced by her sister at a dance, she and Bob became friends, though she actually loved his brother. Indeed, she said she fell in love with Bob's business (at this time he was working as a stonemason) as she didn't

ABOVE: William Forrest married Janet Gibson.
BELOW: Wedding of Bob & Jessie Lowry.
BELOWRIGHT: With Bobby.

want to spend her whole life on the farm! Their marriage certificate says Jessie and Bob were both aged twenty-five, with Bob's occupation recorded as storekeeper. They were married from her parents' residence, Hastings Hall on Western Springs Road, Auckland, on 27 December 1911.

On the Lowry side of the family was our ancestor Mrs Cecil Frances Alexander, who wrote such hymns as 'All Things Bright and Beautiful', 'Once in Royal David's City' and 'There Is a Green Hill Far Away'. Maybe she had seen into the future and this was *our* One Tree Hill, just as someone named Robert Lowry (surely some relation) wrote my favourite song asking 'Shall we gather at the river?', which of course must be *our* Wade River, heritage from my mother's side of the family.

I have some funny memories of these paternal grandparents and great-aunts. One day when I was about nine, coming home from school through the hole in the hedge (the short cut through Jojo's place), I was surprised by an old lady wandering in through our Park gate like a lost sheep. She asked me, in a lilting sort of way, 'Can yer make a cup o' tea, dearie?'

'Yes,' I answered, wishing my mother would come from the house to welcome her or otherwise deal with her. But nobody came, and the old lady stood there staring so strangely at me that I blushed and giggled and couldn't meet her eyes. But she kept persisting with her questions, not letting me past, asking 'And which one are yiz?' So I told her I was Vanna, Bob and Irene's third daughter. And who was she?

'Oi'm yer Great-Aunty Anna, an' I'm afther hearing yer sister won the grand proize in the Art Union. Is that the truth, girlie?' I remembered that Robin had recently won an art contest for a catalogue cover design and had her photo in the *Star*. But the Art Union was another prize (the national lottery) so I didn't immediately guess what the old girl was on about, and muttered 'Dunno . . .', thinking 'Where *is* everyone?' And then she was asking again, 'Can yer make a cup o' tea then, dearie?'

'Of course I can!' Surely everyone could do such a simple thing! And going inside the house to read my new library book, I left her standing sheepishly on the path. But when I saw Robin, who was the only one home, and told her who was out there, she went and made the old lady a cup of tea and offered some biscuits. Later my mother growled at me, 'Why wouldn't you make poor thirsty old Aunty Anna a cup of tea? Robin said you refused to.'

'But, Mummy, I thought she was just asking if I knew how to!' I said sulkily, which my mother thought a huge joke (and a reminder that dim kids need clear instructions!). For the rest of her life, whenever and wherever my mother visited me, she'd come in the door asking, 'Can yer make a cup o' tea, dearie?'

I WAS ALWAYS pleased when told we were to spend the winter holidays at Sunnybrae, the sturdy brick house Grandpa Lowry built at Waihi Beach. Sometimes my big sisters came too. One of my parents would take us down on the train, and once our big brown suitcase got stuck in the luggage rack just as we drew in to Waihi station, where the bus to the beach was waiting. I will always remember my embarrassment when my mother, desperately trying to free the case and haul it down, loudly said her *very worst* swear-word, '*Bugger!*'

From Sunnybrae, there were trips to places like Athenree. Once, travelling somewhere, maybe to visit the old place at Hikutaia, the covered truck we were in got stranded in a creek and we were there half the night while the uncles figured how to get us out. I thought that must be how refugees feel. Another time Grandma took us to visit an old lady we'd seen walking the beach in long black robes. We had thought she was a witch, but she was kind and let us play with her marvellous musical-box and in her house there were china ornaments and swans and ballerinas made of pipe-cleaners and tulle. Grandma spoke with awe of this charming, faded beauty who in her youth had played Shakespeare's Juliet on the Glasgow stage — Grandma loved her Shakespeare.

One time I was at Sunnybrae with Cousin Pam, Aunty Jessie's girl, who was a long-jump champion and also played the piano-accordion. Although I was tone-deaf, Pam kindly let me sing lustily along to songs like 'Oh, my Papa, to me he was so wonderful', 'How much is that doggy in the window?' and 'I love those dear hearts and gentle people who live in my home town'. On Waihi Beach when it was warm enough we enjoyed getting tossed about in the fantastic surf, and one day at low tide discovered a dead and very smelly cow which Grandpa Lowry reckoned was washed over from White Island.

One year at the local hall there was a fancy-dress parade with packets of Rolo sweets as prizes. Robin went as a gypsy, with brass curtain-rings dangling from her ears, a black velvet bolero with sequins over a cream full-sleeved blouse, and a circular skirt in red taffeta. Judy and Cousin Pam were prettily dressed by the aunties in real bridesmaids' frocks. And I remember my costume vividly: a green-stemmed cap, shiny green taffeta bodice, white crepe-paper skirt with a green spot painted in each petal. I was a cute but hefty little snowdrop!

I remember occasions when Grandpa's sisters visited, all closely resembling my Great-Aunty Anna. While they were noisily clattering teacups, drinking, eating and gossiping, I was snuggled down behind the sofa, quiet as a mouse so nobody even knew I was there. Suddenly I was moved to jump up and blurt out my first-ever joke, loudly and boldly. 'Mary had a little lamb, the doctor nearly fainted!' Everyone froze for a long moment while I started going hot pink all over. Then Grandma burst out laughing and nearly choked on a mouthful of tea and pikelet, and the others patted her on the back, all tittering and red-cheeked. It took me years to live this down, eh.

I loved Sunnybrae, with its neatly white-painted car-tyre gardens containing purple petunias planted all along the driveway. And how I loved my big fat Grandma! When I grew up I wanted to be comfy, smiling and weigh twenty stone just like her. I enjoyed climbing up on Grandma's wide lap, for right in the middle of her forehead she had this lump she called her 'wen'. If you reached up a tentative finger to give this wen an exploratory poke she'd make sudden loud oinking noises and scare you half to death. I felt sad when she had it removed.

I loved my Irish Grandpa too. He 'had the gift of the gab', had 'kissed the Blarney Stone'. He knew some wicked jokes (when he thought we girls weren't around). At meals he'd ask if you wanted a big piece of bread, then he'd hand you the whole loaf. If you got wise and asked for a small bit, you'd be passed one breadcrumb. In the photo over the page he's in the middle of renovating our old house at One Tree Hill, to a design by Vernon Brown. At Waihi Beach Grandpa Lowry built sturdy little baches with names like Lupin Villa. He also grew huge vegetables in sand among the lupins, and I loved to watch him working in the garden on fine days.

Lulled by sun and the heady smell of lupins, you might hear stories of his early life. How he came to New Zealand on the *Gothic* in 1904, with his parents James and Mary Lowry, from Binion Hill, St Johnston, near Letterkenny

ABOVE: The Binion Hill farm they left behind, house to the left, barns to the right.

in County Donegal. Nine of his twelve brothers and sisters came too, though Lizzie, who'd married a McClintock, stayed behind, and Anna and Sam came later. His parents bought a farm at Hikutaia township for £22 an acre, a record price at that time.

Grandpa Lowry was their second son, and at the age of sixteen started work at one pound a week for the Alley Brothers, who owned about a thousand acres of land. He then did bushwork with a bullock team, bringing huge kauri logs down off the ranges to horse-drawn timber wagons which took them to Hikutaia Creek or the Waihou River to be towed to Auckland. After that he worked as a goldminer at Komata Reefs for a year, contracted to do single-handed drilling, averaging about one pound a ton of quartz, and it was here he earned his first £100. For a while he helped on the family milk-round in Paeroa, then returned to Hikutaia to build a house for his future wife and children. He also built a store, where he handled large quantities of kauri gum, at a price of around £140 a ton. He supplied the miners at Maratoto with groceries twice weekly as well as doing some carting for the mining company. And he was the first contractor to carry mail from Hikutaia to Whangamata, which he did every Friday as it worked in with his grocery delivery. He became involved in St Mary's Anglican Church, built in Hikutaia in 1914. Bert Alley gave the section for it and Grandpa's mother, who had a legacy from

BELOW: Grandpa Lowry at work.

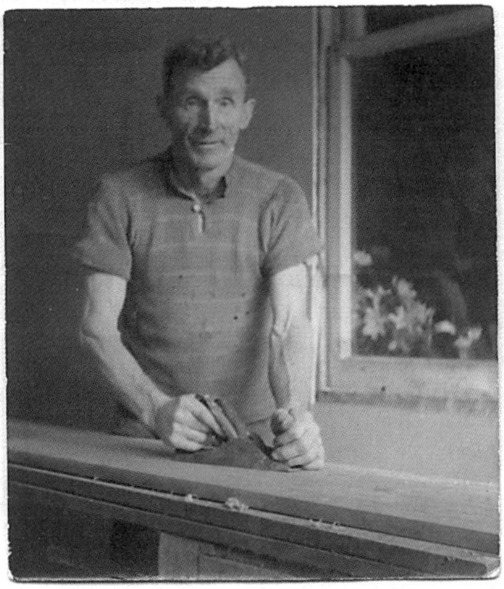

BELOW: Grandma at 96

MARY & JAMES LOWRY WITH FAMILY IN FRONT OF 'LAURISTON'
Bobby Lowry 4th child from left; front row right his father Bob with baby Alex, mother Jessie standing behind them; the rest are Trembaths, Keelings, Durbins, other Lowrys.

Bert's father, gave this money towards the building. Grandpa enjoyed serving on the vestry, built the communion table and prayer desk, and carved the quirky eagle on the lectern.

Near the end of the First World War he sold the business and took over his father's farm of 148 acres on the Maratoto Road, where he and Jessie dairy-farmed for eighteen years. How ironic that Grandma had not got her wish of escaping farm life by marrying a stonemason, after all! Grandpa wrote an account of this in the *Ohinemuri Journal*, where I learned that he had also taken an active part in the Home Guard during the First World War and held a gold medal as life member of the Hikutaia tennis and croquet clubs as well as the bowling club, for which he'd been secretary, and was chairman of the Hikutaia School Committee for several years while his children were attending the school. My father, the oldest son, was born on 17 November 1912, and was followed by Alec, Jessie, Adeline, Bruce and Iris. Two others died at birth. Grandpa served on the Ohinemuri County Council for seventeen years from 1943, and from 1948 did voluntary work for the Waihi Riding, and later Waihi Beach Riding. . . .

Interrupted in his story by Grandma coming to the back door to remind him he was supposed to be digging up some vegetables for dinner, Grandpa dug around till he found a beauty for her, one of his kumara making a meal for six people. Grandma would make yummy roasts of tender meat and mint sauce and gravy to go with the giant kumara, and delicious sweet puddings and scones and sponge cakes with jam and real cream. We were allowed to stay up late around the table with its green tassel-fringed cloth, playing cribbage. Falling asleep between crisp starched sheets, we'd hear the soft soothing sighing of the surf a block away. During May or August holiday storms we'd stay indoors cuddled up with *Girls' Crystal Annual*s and *Reader's Digest*s, or old classics like *Little Women* or *Rebecca of Sunnybrook Farm*. My sister Robin, at Grandma's request, once drew a beautiful sketch of a fancy cup and saucer but, not to be outdone, little Vanna had to have a go too, though my resulting sketch was pathetically lop-sided. Maybe one artist in the family was enough. So, because I'd decided to be a writer when I grew up, as well as twenty stone like her, it was to me Grandma gave her Forrest family heirloom, a wonderful three-volume Shakespeare with embossed blue covers and gorgeous engravings, to keep for my very own. She had a special charm bracelet from which

ABOVE: GRANDMA JESSIE IN FLORAL BEHIND HER PARENTS AT THEIR GOLDEN WEDDING.
BELOW: IRISH GREAT-AUNTS AT LOWRYS' GOLDEN WEDDING IN 1961, WAIHI.

BEHIND: BRUCE, ALEC, BOB LOWRY.
FRONT: JESSIE, GRANDMA, GRANDPA, ADELINE, IRIS

Mr and Mrs R. W. Lowry

request the pleasure of your company

at their Golden Wedding

to be held in the R.S.A. Hall

Waihi Beach

on Sunday 24 December 1961

at 12 noon

R.S.V.P by 9 December
57 Dillon St, Waihi Beach

hung many little tinkling trinkets, each representing a grandchild's birthday, and we were impressed when she could name them all. I was an August pansy, and proud of it.

After Grandpa's retirement we saw less of them, for they shifted to 64 Opaheke Road in Papakura to be near my Uncle Alec and his wife Mollie's family. I visited Grandpa with Mum shortly before he died, aged eighty-four, on 20 August 1971 at Cornwall Hospital, just down the road from our place. I don't know if he remembered us. Several times I visited Grandma Lowry at Selwyn Village in Auckland. On what turned out to be the final visit, I took my daughter and, before going off to find a vase for the flowers we'd brought, I asked Amber to sing a few songs from a musical show she'd been in, *The Caucasian Chalk Circle*, to cheer her great-grandmother up. It was on this visit that Grandma confided to me her regret that she'd 'married the wrong brother'. She died, aged ninety-six, on 19 November 1983, her funeral service being held at St Paul's Anglican Church, Willoughby Street, Paeroa, as was Grandpa's. Both are interred in Paeroa Cemetery.

But, fortunately for me, Grandma did marry Grandpa, so let's get back to their first-born, young Bob. Sent north to stay with his widowed paternal grandmother at 22 Arthur Street, Onehunga, Bob was a scholarship boy at Auckland Grammar. Here he met up with Denis Glover, in whose autobiography, *Hot Water Sailor*, he gets an honourable mention:

> However, at Auckland Grammar School I fell among people of rare talent. I hope every schoolboy does, and recognises whatever talent his friends have. It was there, in my own form, that I met Bob Lowry. Bob Lowry had then a passion for printing and for printing types. We started off with an unofficial form magazine laboriously pencilled out — to the detriment of our homework — and we called this paper *La Vérité*. It was passed round the room during form for nothing. We circulated it out of the goodness of our own hearts. There was only one copy and that went the rounds....
>
> It was after I had left the school that Bob Lowry developed his technique of not merely writing, but of printing on an old proofing press, the form magazine. It rapidly involved him, not for the last time, in trouble with authorities.

Despite belonging to St David's Boy Scout Troop in Khyber Pass, and attending dancing classes run by a formidable lady at Pembridge in Symonds Street, where white gloves were worn, Bob was always larking about, the hub of any mischief. Having won a Lissie Rathbone Scholarship in English and history, he enrolled at Auckland University College and was soon to meet Irene Cornes in Wellington.

MY MOTHER TOLD me that her maternal grandfather, Thomas Percy, was a carpenter whose father had been a farmer. Tom arrived in Auckland in 1884, from County Antrim, Ireland. In 1885, aged twenty-five, he married his nineteen-year-old cousin, Mary Matilda. Her father, William Robert Ellison, had arrived in New Zealand in 1864. He was the first schoolteacher at the Matakana School near Warkworth, but gave up teaching to buy a grocer's shop in Auckland on the corner of Tilden Street and Parnell Road. After his death in 1893 Tom and Matilda (known as Tilly) took over the shop, but later moved to St George's Bay Road and Tom worked as a builder. In 1913 they purchased a 75-acre farm on the Wade River (now known as the Weiti) north of Auckland. The farm became known as Percy's Point, and here they ran chooks, a sheepdog that chased the chooks, and a dozen cows. The only way in was by sea, and the Silverdale steamer came once a week to pick up the cream for the factory.

Their eldest daughter, my grandmother, was Esther Mary (known as May), born in 1886 in Collingwood Street, Ponsonby, the family then moving to Russell Street in Parnell. She was followed by Alexander (known as Alec), Irene (known as Rene), William (known as Bill) and Noel. May attended Prince Albert College near the top of Queen Street till the age of fifteen, where she was taught painting by Kennett Watkins, and continued lessons while working in her parents' grocery. Her next teacher was Charles Goldie, who she reckoned went mad, but was quite good as a teacher. She was later a student of Bessie Blomfield, daughter of Charles Blomfield of the Pink-and-White Terraces fame. Gran believed we 'came over with William the Conqueror', were descended from Lord Nelson, and a distant relative was Harry Percy, who was, of course,

immortalised by Shakespeare as Henry IV's friend Hotspur. By the time her parents retired to Percy's Point, May had set aside her art to marry George Henry Cornes, and raise their own family: Joyce, my mother Irene, Eric and Althea.

My mother's father, George Cornes, was born in 1897 to Scottish farmers at Te Mata, John and Mary, who also had one daughter, Ethel, and five other sons, Johnnie, Willie, Albert, Jack and Tom. Young George attended Auckland College and became a customs officer. In his spare time he was a violinist in the Bohemian Orchestra, a builder of baches and boats, and a sailor. His 26-foot mullet boat, the *Sybil,* was a favourite in the Auckland Regatta of 1880. Tom Percy, May's father, owned the neighbouring boatshed in Mechanics Bay, and apparently George proposed to the beautiful May when he was carrying her out to his boat, declaring that if she refused him he would drop her in the water. As she was wearing new boots of which she was very proud, and didn't want them spoiled by a saltwater dunking, she had to accept the proposal.

George Henry, 2nd from right.

BELOW: Irene, Eric, Gran, Althea, Pop Cornes

'Pop' Cornes, as we all knew him, also loved photography, and was presented on his retirement with a wonderful Rolleicord camera (which I have still). It was he who took the photo of Irene and Bob (below) at her brother Eric's wedding to Betty Preston-Thomas. (Eric was his mother's 'golden boy' and distinguished himself as the New Zealand Major in Charge of Communications during the Second World War, before dying of a brain tumour.) Pop, a gentle man who seemed content pottering around in his carpenter's apron fixing things for Gran, sadly went steadily deafer. Although he would turn off his hearing aid, I remember he would miraculously hear Gran when she softly mentioned the word 'chocolate'. My friend Norah took me to visit him in the Argyle Street rest-home shortly before his death in 1956, and I will never forget the look of frustration and sadness he gave me when I popped a chocolate into his mouth and the juice dribbled down onto his pyjamas.

Note that, even though dressed up in this photo, Bob has that little tuft of hair at the back, even then refusing to conform, and is wearing a buttonhole of wild honeysuckle and his tie crooked. After their own marriage, Irene and Bob set up together in their first flat at 15 Sentinel Road, Herne Bay. And how Bob loved Irene! Unfortunately, her mother, an upright Presbyterian, did not love Bohemian Bob, and refused to come to their registry office wedding on 9 April 1936.

IRENE & BOB

My mother, Irene Ethel Cornes, was born in Parnell on 11 April 1913, and educated at Epsom Girls' Grammar and Wellington Girls' College. The Cornes family would go for holidays to their bach at the Wade. Before her final illness, Irene wrote down for me, and all her descendants, how Percy's Point and land behind it (now Stillwater) was bought by her grandfather from James Graham in the year of her birth. Her grandparents and Uncle Noel worked on this farm for many years, and Aunt Rene for four years.

> The boaties knew it as Percy's Point, where they could buy milk whenever they were anchored in the Wade River on their way to, or back from, other parts of the Gulf. The Percy grandchildren spent many school holidays there swimming off the point, rowing the boats, being taken for picnics to Tiri or Long Bay or Shakespear Beach in the yacht *Dawn*, eating plums and apples from the orchard up in the valley, or watching their grandparents and uncle attending to the farm chores. They watched their grandmother churning the butter, cooking on the wood-stove, feeding the hens and gathering the eggs, or catching (with the help of Ted, the farm dog) a non-laying fowl, chopping its head off, plucking it, dressing it, and cooking it for Christmas dinner or a picnic. They watched their grandfather and uncle milking the cows, hand-separating the cream, growing pumpkins, making hay, ploughing some of the easier land and turning up pieces of kauri gum which the grandchildren helped to scrape, or grubbing the gorse and blackberry in an everlasting battle on the hills where now the owners of the many houses grow roses and cut their lawns with motormowers. On the hills opposite, grass-clad down towards the mouth of the river, a tree-planting scheme was organised during the Depression by an Auckland lawyer, Bruce Scott. The pines and gum-trees, planted in the 1930s by the unemployed, now flourish and beautifully clothe these hills.

Access to Percy's Point, in the early days, was by the Northern Steamship Company's coastal steamers, the *Omana* or the *Orewa*, which sailed from Auckland to Silverdale, arriving there at high tide, and later by the launch *Masport*. The only available access by road was, until 1934, along the Whangaparaoa Peninsula, then turning off onto a side road leading to the top of the

How Grandma Percy makes bread

$\frac{1}{2}$ cake compressed yeast (Dominion)
6 cups flour (about) 2 sifters
2 teasp. salt
2 " sugar

Put about 5 cups flour in basin & make a hole in the middle. Dissolve yeast in $\frac{3}{4}$ pint warm water & pour in hole (Sugar & salt are mixed with flour). Stir enough of the flour into liquid to make a batter (leave rest round outside) Set in warm place till it bubbles up. (about $\frac{1}{2}$ hour). Mix in rest of flour & knead it in till it stops sticking to the hands. Leave to rise till about double its bulk (1 to 2 hrs depending on temperature) Cover with double cloth. Lif out on floured board. Slash with knife to let big bubbles out. Shape into loaves & put in greased tins. Let rise (covered with cloth) till about double the bulk. (Not too much as this makes it coarse) Bake $\frac{3}{4}$ to 1 hour depending on size of loaves. Have oven hot at first (till it begins to brown) then lower heat a bit to finish.

Grandma made wholemeal bread using $\frac{2}{3}$ wholemeal & $\frac{1}{3}$ white flour.

A nob of butter can be added

Milk can be used instead of warm water.

WRITTEN OUT BY
IRENE LOWRY

hill opposite Percy's Point. Then came a walk down to the riverbank and a lift across to the point by Tom Percy in his 11-foot dinghy. Mail had to be collected by walking several kilometres to the post office and store above Arkles Bay, but provisions for the house and farm came by boat from Auckland. The dinghy or punt met the steamer or launch in midstream, off-loaded its cans of cream or sacks of pumpkins, and received sacks of sugar, flour, wheat, pollard, bran, etc. in return.

Water and walking were the essential elements of access to Percy's Point. Visitors sometimes came by taking a bus to Deep Creek, walking across the Okura River at low tide, then across the vast expanse of hard mud in front of Dacre's Beach and up the Wade River, across mudflats and points, till they arrived at Percy's. My mother wrote:

> The young people used to row down the river on Saturday nights, anchor the dinghy opposite Gum-tree Point, and walk about three miles to a dance at Arkles Bay. For a family picnic at Red Beach, we used to row up the river to Bayley's Landing, tie up the dinghy, walk up the hill through the farm, pick up Cicely Bayley, go across Whangaparaoa Road, and down through the paddocks to the eastern end of the beach (beautiful sand and sea unpopulated by anyone but us).

Around 1934 the dirt road running from East Coast Road to Noel Percy's farm was metalled and made usable, except for the last few hundred metres, which later took it through to Stillwater Point. In 1936 the farm at Percy's Point was sold by auction, but Pop Cornes retained the twenty-seven acres further up the river (later Cashmore's property) on which Tom Percy had built a house which was almost a replica of his house on Percy's Point. This property was used for several years by the Cornes family and their friends during holidays. Grandpop planned to retire there and run cattle on the land but, when attempting to transport a bull (for the heifers he already had) by barge from Shakespear's Beach, he broke his leg very badly and in 1940 he sold the property.

However, he retained half an acre on Messengers Road, putting it in my grandmother's name. She told us how this land was originally acquired. 'My father was up the river building a house there and he damaged some trees belonging to the next farm. The farmer came along and was going to sue him to

The Auction of Percy's Point

pay for it, and my father says, "How much do you want?", and that's how he got that bit of land. He bought the land that he'd damaged the trees on.' This section became May and George's, and George built baches there for Irene and Bob, and for Aunty Althea and husband, lawyer Jack Northey. Their two eldest, Richard and Jill, were my playmates every summer, and there were many happy outings to gather cockles at Matakatia or picnics at Red Beach or Hatfields (see photo opposite, guess who was grumpy with toothache?).

When we were kids it took half a day to get to the Wade, waiting in Pop's car for hours in the vehicular ferry queue, entertained by flower-sellers and buskers. We'd stay the six long hot weeks of the summer school holidays, while the fathers came up at weekends or special occasions. Sometimes we'd tie the Dumbles' dinghy on behind our little dinghy, which was tied to our big dinghy, and Pop or Uncle Jack would attempt to start the outboard motor. This never seemed to be immediately amenable, which Pop and my uncle did not find amusing, but finally the cursing would work and our cavalcade would pass in a dignified fashion out to the mouth of the river at Gum-tree Point. I liked to sit right up on the bow of the big dinghy pretending I was Saucy Nancy, the figurehead from a favourite book about scarecrow Worzel Gummidge. We helped to gather cockles and drag the mullet nets, enjoying the bounty of snapper and flounder. At dawn we went out picking mushrooms from the paddocks, and fried them in butter for breakfast.

But the brothers-in-law had fallings-out. After the Northey twins, Glenda and Bruce, were born, the section was becoming too small for both families and in 1960, before the birth of their youngest child, Tom, the Portheys bought land on the Coromandel. May gifted the half-acre to my mother (on whose death it came to my three sisters and me). So 'the Wade', as we call it (baches, half-acre, river, the whole area), the Wade because of all its history always felt like our mother's place. Our father never seemed quite comfortable there, even on the little holiday time he could spare. Partly this was because our bach was too small for him. There was a small, square dining-living-kitchen room with a coloured-glass window from our old One Tree Hill house. Off this was our parents' room, containing a double bunk with a single (storage) bunk above it. Next to it was the four-bunk girls' room, from which we could hear our father snoring, and Robin from her top bunk could look over the wall into our parents' room. Because of the open plan, though, there wouldn't be

L to R: ROBIN, VANYA, JUDY & IRENE LOWRY; JILL, RICHARD & ALTHEA NORTHEY

ABOVE: ROBIN, JUDY, VANYA IN THE BIG BOAT.

ABOVE: LOWRYS' BACH,
IRENE & THREE GIRLS.
LEFT: RICHARD, JUDY,
VANYA & POP'S VAN.

ABOVE: L & R, May's paintings of Percy's Point
BELOW: Left, John Dumble's painting of Wade river.
BELOW: Right, Robin Lowry's painting of red baches.

anything to see; apparently, if they wanted any conjugal bliss a short walk into the pines was the solution.

But our father wanted to belong there, I know he did. Once, rowing me up-river in the dinghy, he taught me the proper names of birds like the pied shags which I remember to this day, *Phalacrocorax melanoleucos*. Curiously, every time now when I go to the river for my daily row and swim, a lone shag will erupt from the mangroves to come and sit on the sign in the middle of the river that states 'NO JETSKIS NO JETBOATS. BY ORDER'. I like to think it is my father or his spirit keeping his eye on me from wherever he went, just as the group of five ducks, that often appear from nowhere, seem to be the spirits of Robin and my little niece Kirsten and my mother, who all died too soon, and my grandmother May and great-grandmother Tilly, who loved the Wade so much.

With such alarm must they be looking on helplessly, as do we the living, every time the place is threatened: by that Oriental Honeymoon Hideaway

"Sea shell ebb music Wade River sea flows" – JAMES JOYCE

With very best wishes

for Christmas and the New Year, 1954-5

from the Lowry Family

32 Gladwin Road, Epsom, Auckland S.E.3

down our country road; by that ostentatious suburb now crowding out the old Stillwater; by the intractable gorse now covering the best real estate on the point that used to be Percy's orchard, looking towards the Waitemata Harbour. And worst of all are the latest threats at the time of writing: the closure of the marvellous Okura Walkway; and the proposed building of a bloody great toll-bridge which seems to be going ahead despite many residents' concerted protestations, a dreadful scar slashing a swathe across the land and the river, destroying unique wildlife, a community, just so that commuters can cut six minutes off the travelling time from Auckland to that ghastly billionaires' paradise at Gulf Harbour!

Back then, it used to feel weird coming home to One Tree Hill after our hols, for the gardens had turned into a giant wilderness with lawns up to our waists, and the house seemed huge and echoing. It would take a while to get used to all that space. First thing, though, we'd have to help our mother kerosene the floors where our noisy vibrations had woken fleas from their hiding-place in the cracks between boards.

DEWDROPS

Velvet-clad night is ending now her sway;
The countless stars that twinkled high and low
Are fading one by one; and as they go
Each breaks into a million fragments grey
Which, falling softly, wait on earth for day.
And when the waking sun with rosy glow
Peeps smiling o'er the hills, his first rays show
That every plant and leaf and flower is gay
With shimmering pearls; then climbing slowly higher
His bright light catches on each shattered star.
(Men call it dew), to make the fragments gleam
Like priceless jewels, and flash with living fire.
They burn with colour, till the sun afar
Draws them to heaven again upon his beam

—I.C., VI.

PREFECTS.

N. Berry, M. Christie, E. Lenihan, J. Morgan, M. Neill, I. Cornes

Back again to the young Irene, who had finished her school years on a high note. The Wellington Girls' College *Reporter* of 1929 shows her as a prefect, member of the Library Committee, plump-faced beauty photographed with the Moorish Dancers, winner of the Form VI prize for Good Work, third in the senior 50 yards at swimming, second prizewinner of the Hilda Moorhouse Essay Prize, contributor of the poem 'Dewdrops' and story 'The Pot of Gold'. In her final year she won a Junior Scholarship to university. Only rarely, later, did she find time to write a poem, like 'The River'.

But my mother's talent for poetry was almost completely ignored after she met Bob. She worked in a cigarette factory for thirty shillings a week (plus as many fags as she could smoke), and went on to play the role of supportive wife to my father. Although he was the director of every show, together they collected creative people of all kinds around themselves like ants around a honeypot.

THE RIVER.

She feels no comfort on my summer banks -
no longer finds perennial peace
the seasonal stillness I have given to her
for two-score years.
Yet I repeat these age-old patterns -
sink to brown channels and leave
the shining mud busy with crabs,
and rise again inevitably to full-tide,
slide green past boats
cover the rocks, the barnacles and slime,
provide a surface in a hushed lagoon
at evening for her exploring boat.
Has she forgotten the descending peace,
how mangroves, half-submerged,
will whisper underneath her keel?
I smooth my breast, black for the moon's reflection,
race yellow to the sea, burdened with rain and clay -
she looks, and turns away
back to a secret tumult of her own,
tumult not born of wind and current.
Does she not remember how her oars
will drip with phosphorus
slice silver into my skin while her boat carves out
a shining arrow on the motionless black?
She does not come
to find me in the evening:
and even in the full blaze of the afternoon
when I lie blue-green, brimming to the banks,
she brings her body only,
sun-drenched, wading in
from habit, not from love,
and does not feel my blessing -
dries off the tingling salt with heedless towel
among the ferns. She cannot see
past her own present hurt of change and doubt,
and feel the calm
unchanging certainty of ebb and flow.

Irene Lowry

The Phoenix and the Unicorn

BOB'S CAREER STARTED on a high note also. In March 1932 he printed the first of four issues of the infamous *Phoenix* for the Auckland University College Literary Club. As Denis Glover remembered in the Caxton miscellany *Book* 8 (August 1946):

> There were no proof-sheets; for the supply of type only ran to one page at a time. The whole magazine, therefore, was hand-set and printed by one heroic individual, and in several different places at that. It ran to fifty-two pages, demy octavo, and if it is not typographically distinguished it is certainly a triumph over difficulties. With July came Number Two, bearing the grandiloquent imprint: 'Auckland: at the University Press'. It was a tremendous improvement, and is, to my mind, still one of the happiest of Lowry's achievements. The title-page, with the phoenix device in red, and faced by a small lino-cut, makes an instant appeal. The contents list is remarkable for a traditional use of roman caps with italic lower-case in a Caslon Old Face which is also used for the text.

But things never ran smoothly for Bob, as Ron Holloway remembered in *Landfall* 69 (March 1964):

> The character of the chronic undergraduate seemed to settle upon him then, and it remained with him. Beer and bawdiness were essential to this part of his nature. Before the second *Phoenix* was printed, the plant had been taken over by the Students' Association, and with a power-driven platen, was established in a basement room under the Science Building. The chemists let their sinks overflow and much paper was spoilt; and there were stinks. Meanwhile the unemployed rioted in Queen Street, and Bob, like many other students, was enrolled as a special constable and hung up his truncheon behind the printery door. Before long there were more riots, but our Guardian of the Law was already on the side of the Oppressed. In Court, a fellow constable attempted to report Bob's inflammatory words verbatim; from the prisoner the SM heard, 'That, sir, is not my idiom!'

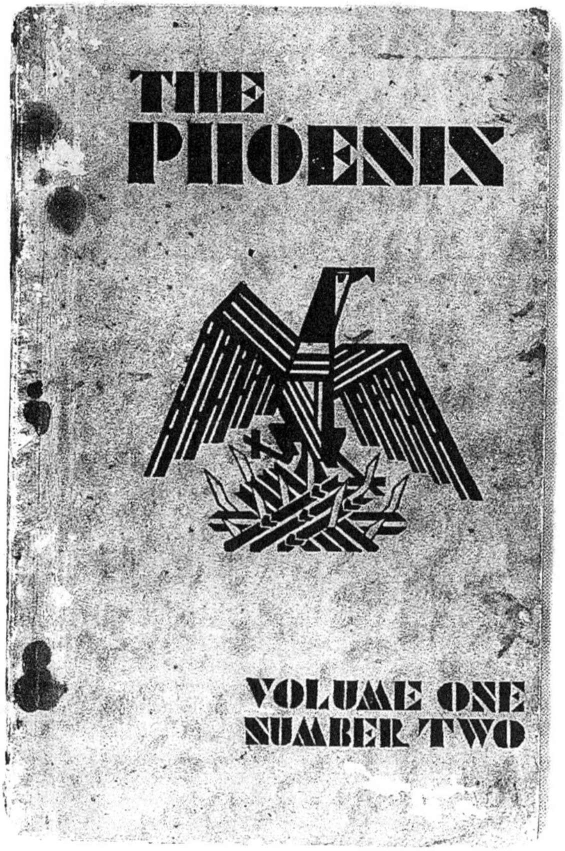

And later in the *New Zealand Observer*, Robin Hyde noted that the court imposed a remarkable two years' probation and 7 pm curfew on Bob for disturbing the peace during the 1934 'Free Speech' rallies.

Glover continued:

> With Volume Two Number One it is a different story. *Phoenix* is now a quattro, and except for a good title-page it is important without being gracious. Chunky two-colour lino-cuts excite little admiration now, and headings are rather bleakly handled in Gill Sans, then a newcomer to these astonished shores. From its exciting cover in large Caslon Old Face (surely the most ruggedly satisfying of all types) Volume Two

> Number Two leads us to expect an old style journal. But we don't get it. The title-page consists of three asymmetrical dollops of Gill Sans, standing round like people who haven't been introduced at a party; and the headings, except on page one, are mean affairs. Initial letters throughout are unsatisfactory, as they always are unless made or trimmed to range exactly with a specified number of lines. This number is at first glance impressive — the lino-cuts are on a yellow paper — and is ingeniously printed on a laid duplicating. Here, then, was *Phoenix* (for after a fourth flight the bird failed to take off again), important not only for what it was but for what it led to. Not writers alone were tentatively stretching their wings, but a typographer.

Holloway takes up the story:

> His Press was already an instrument of propaganda [an unacceptable article had to be pulled at the last minute] . . . And the President of A.U.C. Stud. Ass. Martin Sullivan, later to become Archdeacon of London [and Dean of St Paul's] . . . had to come down to the basement to suppress things. Bob went out before lunch one day, and when he did not come in the following morning I helped myself to the forsaken lunch [a stale sandwich]. . . And continued the machining of Curnow's *Valley of Decision*. The accounts were in confusion, of course . . . Bob admitted that he had bitten off more than he could chew. He had gone to Christchurch.

Glover again, now at the Caxton Club Press in Christchurch, as recorded in *Hot Water Sailor*:

> Anyhow Bob turned up over the long vacation; I still had the press in the basement under the law students' lecture room, and Bob and I set to work manfully to print an eighty-page book, *Little Plays from Maori Legends*, for which we were offered money. We hand-set every page, distributed the type, hand-set another page, and printed them, one at a time. This was until [college rector] Dr Hight drew my attention to the fact that Bob Lowry, having been proscribed by Auckland University

UNICORNS
FOR THE
UNICORN PRESS

College, was *persona non grata* at Canterbury University College.... So we reached the beautiful and farcical situation where I... would be machining busily in the basement — pumping the handle one page at a time on an eight inch by five inch platen press — while Lowry, who had established himself in a 5s a week hutment down the road, would there set up the type and bring it down to Worcester Street. He would wave, shout, and gesticulate furiously in the street outside. I looking through my fake Gothic slit window from the basement, would hurry to receive from without the iron gates the new forme of hand-set type and give him back the one that had already been printed. I don't pretend we made good money, but that job was fun.

Holloway again:

> He left behind a considerable achievement, notably the four issues of *Phoenix*, *A.U.C. Jubilee Book*, which would be a credit to any University Press, and *Kiwi 1932,* its cover beautiful in a simplicity unlike that of any previous issue, and made glorious by Mason's poetry. When Bob returned, Ron Mason set up the Unicorn Press in his own house for the printing of a small edition of his poems collected as *No New Thing*, as austere and disciplined in its hand-set type as the verse demanded. The title page of this book, good in itself, was not properly related to the text, and Bob left a few copies unbound, hoping to complete them in better style. They remain unfinished, a testimonial to his insatiable quest for perfection.

After a short spell at photographer Clifton Firth's studio, the Unicorn shifted to Kitchener Street, where they printed *Lyttelton Harbour* by D'Arcy Cresswell, *Katherine Mansfield* by Arthur Sewell, *Conversation with My Uncle* by Frank Sargeson, and two small things by Robin Hyde. Leaving Ron Holloway and his wife Kay to pay off the debts (and finish printing Rod Finlayson's *Brown Man's Burden*), Bob moved on in 1939 to work on that first hilarious collaboration, *The Sky Is a Limpet*, with chief comrade-in-mischief, Rex Fairburn.

"THE SKY IS A LIMPET"

SPREACH FROM THE PRONE, BY THE RETURNABLE MR SELVEDGE

Lazies & Jellymen :

As Prime Morningstar of this beautiful little commentary it is my pleasure to undress to you a few verbs. Worst of all, I wash to comegrabulate the Godallment on being the boast godallment in the wild we live in.

We are the Gobblement, and we mean to gullible this contrary. We are growing to make all stratospheres of the community hoppy, onwards and uppishness into a void hurting moneybody. We are dizzy bilking a compunitive parody of the Specific, and we are not going to alloy ourselves to be circumverted by anybodies. Now then.

We see be four years today the spentacle of property in the maddest of plenty. We intent to romedy this. The ambitional social surpluses we are constiplating will convolvulus in higher intaxication. It is the cistern that is wrung & nought the indivisible. We have been called

idealess and evasionaries. I reply with all fours of which I am culpable that we are not versionary, and that on the country

our anemones are reaggravationaries, who wash to embarrass us, and who are merely out to pretext worsted undervests. Of what do they accurse us? Do they say we are not honours? Do they twistion our intorquity? We are doing a bust to falfoul the mendit we were govern by the purple, and the purple wool decide at the parrot box weather is bad or goodbye. Now then.

The sadistics of production show how nursery it is for the devilment of our sick and dreary industries to be putsched fordward, and we must bill the nation. Our local malefacturers must be incorriged, and we must do our boast to increase the voluble prediction of goods. I have recently made a tour of expection of our fictories, and it is quite fascistmaking to see how they are crowing by lips and bonds.

Will there be a Bludget circus now then? As you have herd in a rodeo breadcast by my cowlick the Master of Finesse wee hope there will be a surplice on the Budgie, and if knot we shall have to burrow interminally or obtain some overseers, butt at present it all deep ends.

Sins the Jumble Evection of 1935, at which we war successpool, we have been botching devilopments in foreign afires & we are somewhit consigned abort the future. For the gyration of our period in offings we shall take port in all confluences and disgustions on whirled affairs. We owe in continual constultification with Histrajesty's Garblement in Got Bitten.

If we wool all go to gather and discussion our difficulties, I am skirting

everything in the gordian will be lively. We are upstage men, we sore onwards and upstairs, we pie through the sky high up into the crowds, and no poor on earth can bestir us from getting what we wont. We have learnt our votes and are going forwards to fine old figtree. Fly up in the sky we will cling to oar high idols of serve us. What the cloud wants we will give them, and cling to the sky ideals like it lumpit on the rocks or fly on the ceiling. Now then.

At The Radiant Hall

CHRIST CHVRCHE

To Commence on

SATVRDAY THE TENTH FEBRVARY, MDCCCCXLV

for a Seafon of Seven Evening Performances

& Three Matinees

The Tragicall Hiftorie of HAMLET, *Prince of Denmarke*

TO BE FOLLOWED BY

The Tragœdy of OTHELLO, *The Moore of Venice*

*

By William Shakefpeare

As they have beene Diverfe Times enacted by the

CAVNTERBVRY VNIVERSITIE COLLEDGE DRAMA SOCIETIE

in the Citties of Chrift Chvrche, Avckland,

VVellington & Dvnedin

*

PRODVCED BY NGAIO MARSH

The Tour Directed by D. D. O'CONNOR

BY THIS TIME my mother had given birth to Robin, at St Helen's Hospital on 24 February 1938. During 1985, Robin's last year, when she was in Carrington Hospital suffering from a brain tumour and I had given her an old exercise book for her memoirs, she remembered:

> My mother had to mop the floors of the hospital corridors very energetically in order to start the labour more quickly as I was two weeks overdue, and made my debut in this world weighing in at a hefty 9 lbs, subsequently claiming big bones as the reason for always since then being a large girl. My parents shortly moved to Otorohanga, where I believe we suffered extreme cold; me being a tiny waif with 'big bones' in a white nightgown, wandering about in the early mornings being potty-trained. My bottom, exposed to endless hours on an enamel chamber, must have resembled a baboon's. There were chilblains too, and no fuel, as it was mid-winter, and the war was well under way. We would go at Christmas-time to my paternal grandfather's farm at Hikutaia in the Thames valley, where I was the pampered darling of innumerable aunts, uncles and cousins, healthy outdoor farming types with the inevitable wicked Irish sense of humour.
>
> From Otorohanga, where we were staying I believe with the Anso family, we moved to Ngataki up north in the gum fields. My father was appointed 'Infant Mistress' at the little two-teacher school. In those days a Training College student did a year's country service before entering College proper. The local population was almost entirely Maori, all with hearts of pure gold, or possibly kauri gum, who used to leave a few fish and a bunch of parsley or a few turnips and swedes on the doorstep of our corrugated iron shack every morning. The Maoris used to call their children ambitious names such as Dargaville and Pohutukawa. One of my father's duties was to give his Maori pupils their dose of Cod Liver Oil each morning against the prevalent TB and as they were very reluctant he was often to be seen chasing them across the paddocks with a tablespoon in one hand and a bottle of Cod Liver Oil in the other! As it was wartime he used to do a lot of his teaching in a shelter shed ...

'Infant Mistress' with wife & baby; home in Ngataki

Rocco the Rooster

He woke me early every morning. Whenever I met him I threw bricks at him. We became very good friends. He would have made a lovely dinner if I could have thrown straight. He had 17 wives. Doesn't he look silly ?

"Let me have a little book with the insects in it. Oh I do want the book of it—I want in it to be a horse and a house and a flower and a snake and a girl. I would like you to have it done, the book, after the war is over. Would you like a little horse in the book too — I do mean a donkey ?"

ROBIN

Here's your Horse

His name is Ferdie, and he's very strong. He eats grass, and oats when he can get them. He pulls a cart up to the camp and takes the scraps away for the pigs. But sometimes he just stands in the paddock. He likes that far better.

Billy le Bouc

This is a little French goat. The little boys and girls love to play with him. They tie him up to coconut palms, so that he won't run away. He has a bell on his neck, and if he gets loose they can hear where he is and catch him.

A book for 'Robin-a-bobbin'

After this Ngataki stint the Lowry family went back to Auckland, where my second sister, Judith, was born in 1940. In a memoir written at my request, friend Patrick Dobbie remembered:

> 1941 was Bob's second year at Teachers' Training College. I helped him print the College magazine. His College [printery] was in the Art Department; a small hand-fed treadle platen, my first sight of a printing machine. The whole printing process intrigued me, especially after I had motorised the platen. The press was soon shifted to a cubby-hole of a basement room under the stage of the assembly hall and there Bob and I spent the rest of the year publishing/editing page by page what was probably one of ATTC's most elegant *Manukas*. Bob told me once that he really wanted to write, not print. I must add that our College work, that for which we were paid more or less a living wage, suffered grievously. Bob cut many of the initials and decorations to be printed in colour, and much in the text was evidence of Lowry humour.

EARLY IN 1942 Bob had been called up and posted to the artillery. Robin remembered:

> Bob was off to New Caledonia as a commissioned officer in the New Zealand Army. He held the rank of 2nd Lieutenant. He never saw any active combat while he was over there but . . . he was greatly attracted to the local French girls although he complained that their breath always smelt of garlic. I wrote him a letter saying that I wanted him to make me a book after the war was over and that the book should have in it a house and a snake and a flower and a girl. He set to work and hand-cut some illustrations in lino and hand-set the script in Gill sans-serif, printing the result on buff hand-made paper. Four pages were done. Many years later I got Pat Dobbie to make a cover and collated the whole thing, hand-stitching it together in the traditional way with linen thread. The finished copies I gave away to favoured friends as

> Christmas gifts. It was a limited edition of 100 copies and I played a typical Lowry trick and numbered each copy number one so that every recipient thought that they had the special favour!

On 10 June 1943 (two months before my birth) Bob wrote to his sister Adeline that New Caledonia was a backward country but

> there are plenty of coconut palms and banana trees about — also plenty of oranges, mandarins & limes (like very small lemons but absolutely full of juice). Then sometimes we see a turtle at the beach, with its eggs packed in dozens like soft very white ping-pong balls about a yard down in the sand. It's all very interesting — but they can have it for mine. A.E.W.S. stands for Army Education and Welfare Service. We give the soldiers booklets about world affairs, run films, a concert party, the *Kiwi* newspaper, help them to carry on their studies while in camp . . . also run a library service. . . . The job I do is alright but still too much damned work. It's getting better: if I hadn't caught dengue fever, we might have got things right by now. If you do see the kids when you get your holidays, I can't hear too much about them. Iris tells me a lot that Irene doesn't mention.

Although the printery had proved more attractive than the lecture room, Bob managed to graduate with a BA from Auckland University College in 1943. When he was demobilised in 1944, he resumed teaching at Seddon Memorial Technical College. Here he taught 'art, design and layout, bookbinding, the chemistry of printing, compositors' work, and letterpress machining' (*Seddonian*, 1945). Staff and pupils appreciated him, till lateness became a problem because of the demand for his private printing and the demands of a growing family. In 1940 this poem had appeared in Denis Glover's *Cold Tongue*:

> ON A DILATORY PRINTER
> When the Last Trump gives forth its sound
> And angels don the jury look
> Lowry will keep God hanging round
> For proof-sheets of the Judgement Book.

On his return Bob had set up the Pelorus Press, with a printing press in a garden shed by the gate at 32 Gladwin Road. Pat and Mary Dobbie were sharing the house with us by this time and Pat helped Bob in the printery, 'working on pamphlets with the emphasis on fine typography. A loan of 100 pounds from [Honey Haigh's brother, the entrepreneur] Dan O'Connor enabled Bob to buy a second-hand press, another platen, this time a semi-automatic, and some type . . . highlights being *Speaking for Ourselves,* edited by Sargeson, *What's Wrong with Broadcasting* by Ormond Wilson, *Whims of a WAAF* by Rosalie Seddon, and Bob and Rex Fairburn's *How to Ride a Bicycle in Seventeen Lovely Colours*.'

Of this last, Pat Dobbie recalled: 'I think we printed 2000 copies, and each of the five folios and cover had to be hand-fed eight times through the machine, to say nothing of the endless folding and refolding and refolding and refolding . . . my interest in this venture steadily leaked away . . . we finished the damn thing and I undertook a kind of hitchhiking journey south as far as Christchurch peddling it to booksellers. . . . I think it was offered for five shillings.'

PI R Squared and Popery

In Sir Charles Scarborough's time, Dr. Batchcroft (the head of Caius College) would visit the boyes chambers, and see what they were studying; and Charles Scarborough's genius let him to the mathematics, and he was wont to be reading of Clavius upon Euclid. The old Dr. had found in the title "e Societate Jesu" and was much scandalized at it. Said he, "By all means let us leave off this author, and read Protestant mathematical bookes."

—John Aubrey

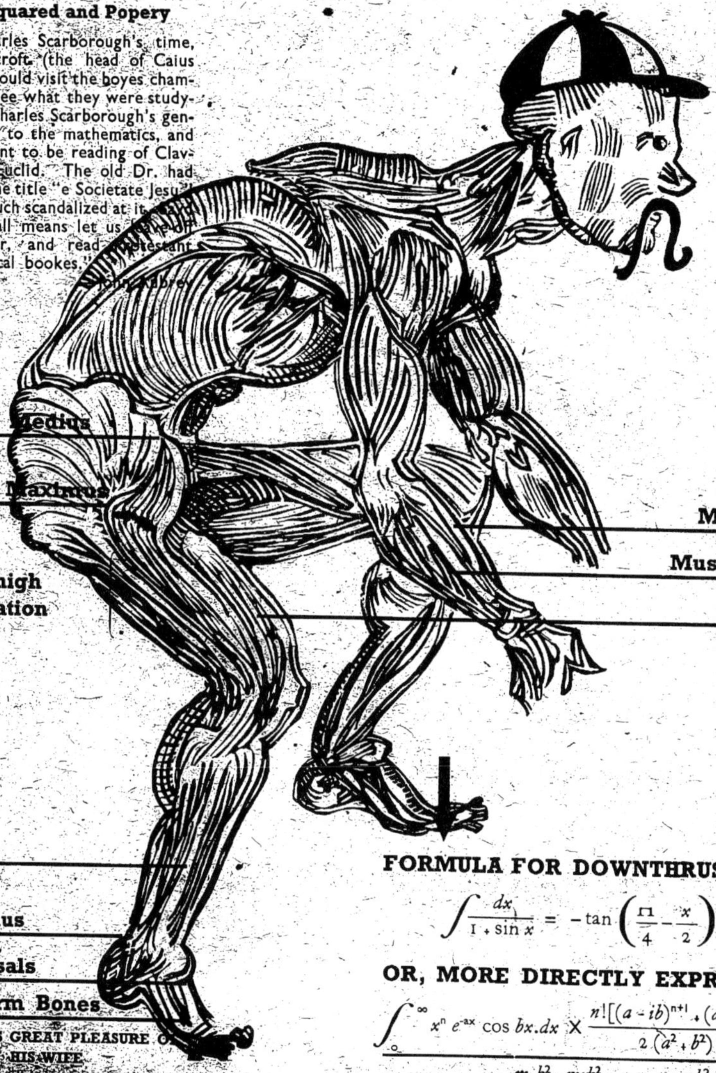

FORMULA FOR DOWNTHRUST ACTION

$$\int \frac{dx}{1 + \sin x} = -\tan\left(\frac{\pi}{4} - \frac{x}{2}\right) + C$$

OR, MORE DIRECTLY EXPRESSED,

$$\frac{\int_0^\infty x^n e^{-ax} \cos bx.dx \times \frac{n![(a - ib)^{n+1} + (a + ib)^{n+1}]}{2(a^2 + b^2)^{n+1}},\ a > 0}{\frac{m_1 k_1^2 + m_2 k_2^2 + \dots + m_n k_n^2}{m_1 + m_2 + \dots m_n}}$$

where $\left(\frac{dx}{dt}\right)_1$ is the value of $\frac{dx}{dt}$ at (x_1, y_1, z_1).

PEPYS HAS GREAT PLEASURE OF HIS WIFE

At noon I home to dinner with my poor wife, with whom now-a-days I enjoy great pleasure in her company and learning of Arithmetique.

—SAMUEL PEPYS

WARNING! The copyright of this valuable plate is held by Dumbbell's Postal College. Reproduction is expressly forbidden in all countries party to the Berne Convention.

DUMBBELL'S POSTAL COLLEGE

"Mr Everyman's University"

SHORT COURSE IN BICYCLE-RIDING Lesson 1

It is necessary for the Tyro to realise at the outset that the essential aim in Bicycle-riding is to maintain an erect position, while at the same time propelling the Bicycle in a forward direction by pedal action.

PROCEDURE: (1) Take up a position on the left-hand or south side of the Bicycle, about half-way along it.

(2) Grasp the handle-grips of the Bicycle firmly, by manipulation of the flexor and extensor muscles of the hands, the right-hand grip in the right hand, the left-hand grip in the left hand.

(3) Place that part of the fascia of the left foot covering the junction point of the cuneiform and metatarsal bones on the pedal in closest proximity to your person.

(4) With the ball of the right foot pressed firmly against the ground, perform smartly a forward propulsive movement, immediately afterwards pronating the right thigh, swinging the right leg over, and placing your seat on that of the Bicycle.

(5) Place that part of the fascia of the RIGHT foot covering the junction of the cuneiform and metatarsal bones on the right-hand pedal, and proceed to rotate pedals rapidly, with the feet, in a forward direction. (The pedal action will have a clockwise motion when viewed from the right-hand side of the Bicycle, and an anti-clockwise motion — known technically as "widdershins" — when viewed from the left-hand side. As it is not possible for you to take either of these views when actually riding the Bicycle, it is suggested that you get some other person to check this action for you.) The pedal action is performed by the alternate flexion and extension, in each leg, of the junctions of the tibia, the fibula and the astragalus, and of the femur and the tibia.

The riding of the common Bicycle, or Velocipede, is simplicity itself once these few fundamental principles have been firmly grasped.

Having completed the evolutions described above, you will find yourself moving rapidly forward. To turn and change direction, all that is necessary is to rotate the handle-bars to the right or left (north or south) as the case may be. The Bicycle may be brought to a dead stop by applying the brakes. The position of these on the Bicycle will have been indicated to you by the person from whom you purchased it.

Repeat this procedure until you have gained confidence, and are able to manoeuvre the Bicycle in any direction you wish without falling off.

WARNING!

These lessons are and remain the property of Dumbbell's Postal College, in whom the copyright is vested. They must not be shewn, talked about, lent or given away to any other person nor quoted recited or sung in any public place for profit, nor copied, either in whole or in part, whether in manuscript or by any other means whatsoever, without the expressed prior consent of the Proprietors, given in writing, and on payment of a substantial fee to be determined on application.

Other ATTRACTIVE DUMBBELL POSTAL COURSES

ROLLER-SKATING

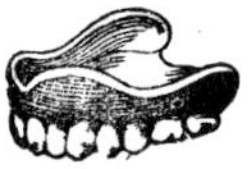

PUBLIC SPEAKING

BOOGIE-WOOGIE

COOKERY

LOGIC AND ETHICS

NAVIGATION

TELEVISION

BUSINESS PSYCHOLOGY

"THE LAURELS", FOURTH AVENUE, MIDDLEBURG

16th June.

Dr E. Dumbbell,

c/o Dumbbell's Postal College.

Dear Sir,

I am sorry to put pen to paper again and give you bad news but I am still falling off my Bicycle every time. It just feels like somebody pushes me though of course nobody does. Please will you tell me if I ought to lean my head and body over to one side when I feel I am falling and if this will help.

Yours obediently,

Alfred E. Wardle.

P. S. I tried getting on the off-side of the Bicycle also turning the handle bars left and right but it doesn't work.

P. P. S. My wife still doesn't like your letterhead.

Old house at One Tree Hill

The Lowrys' House is coming down
And Vernon Brown is going to town.

Last looniest loveliest party in the
Old Landmark, Saturday June 19

Bring no more grog than can be
conveniently stowed in a taxi

No coming before 7.30

A small group of Lee Johnson paintings
on view, including some work in progress

Cockels and mussels for supper!

I WAS FIVE YEARS old in 1948 when the old house at One Tree Hill was rebuilt, but I don't remember much of this, as I was sent to stay with the Dobbies at the Wade, where Pat had taken a job as shepherd to Old Man Cashmore. Grandpa Lowry was helped in the rebuilding at One Tree Hill by Pop Cornes and by the startling-looking White Russian Bill Anso, my Pedlar man, the source of one of Sargeson's best-known stories, 'The Hole that Jack Dug'. By this time the tradition was well established of whimsical Christmas cards and invitations designed by Bob and decorated with assorted old blocks.

ABOVE: Mum among renovations.

ABOVE: Robin & Vanya, old house. BELOW: Gran, new house.

On the walls of the renovated house were hung paintings by friends. I remember Joan Smith's oil painting of me dressed in green, and her sister-in-law May Smith's 'Weird woman in green with wonky eyes', as I thought of it, but actually *Characterisation in Colour*, painted in 1941 and now in the Auckland City Art Gallery. Other artist friends had solo shows around the walls, such as Keith Patterson, Eric Lee-Johnson and Dennis Knight Turner. And the rambling house, with its large living room, garden and spare bedrooms, became The Party House, as taxi-drivers and neighbours came to know all too well.

Pharmacist George Gunn remembers what he called the 'Bloomsbury Set' parties.

> You were surely one of the chosen if you were invited to them. The stimulation of alcohol led to the most scintillating topics of conversation. One evening I shall never forget. Jennie and I picked up Bob and Irene from Epsom to attend a party at Sam and Moll Leathem's place. . . . At suppertime, standing by the table and helping himself to some salad, Bob launched out on his 'Ode to a Cucumber' [now unfortunately lost]. He wove it round the then current Lysenko controversy. Lysenko, a Soviet biologist of dubious scientific qualifications nevertheless had the right political connections; he was a protégé of the Soviet leader, Stalin. As such, whatever his colleagues thought of him, he could do no wrong. He propounded some bizarre biological theory that was taken as gospel in the USSR but greeted with some derision in the rest of the world. Bob's 'Ode' was one of the most brilliant spontaneous renditions I have ever heard.

When did things begin to go wrong for the marriage? Was it only cheap plonk that destroyed all that was good about Bob and Irene's life? Was it his recklessness with money, leading to business failures and later bankruptcy, which meant Irene had to go out to work, first as assistant to Professor Laurie Holt, then as clerk at the law school library. Or was it a combination of these plus Bob's jealousy of rivals for Irene's affection?

The demands of four stroppy daughters can't have helped, for we would be joined by Brigid in 1953, as commemorated in this Fairburn verse, later published in *Poetry Harbinger* 1958:

FRIENDLY GREETINGS FROM

THE REHABILITATED LOWRY

FAMILY AT CHRISTMAS AND

THE NEW YEAR 1948-49

32 GLADWIN ROAD EPSOM AUCKLAND

POEM ADDRESSED TO MR ROBERT LOWRY
ON THE OCCASION OF THE BIRTH OF HIS FOURTH DAUGHTER

How lucky we are Mr Lowry,
to live in the land of the kauri;
just think what, between us,
our commerce with Venus,
would have cost in the days of the dowry.

JUDY, BRIGID, VANYA

Monday night.

What am I going to do? And who should I consider most when I'm working it out? – apart from myself I mean (because I must be ~~happy~~ satisfied with any course of action if I'm to carry it through.) I can't any longer watch Bob go on drinking and letting the Press go to pieces (what else can be happening there when he spends so little time working?) And I'm so conscious of the sense of guilt that he must have, and that must grow bigger & darker as the days drift to weeks & the weeks to months that I can't even feel like doing the ordinary nagging & arguing that I suppose is the normal thing for a wife to do. And anyway I hate the thought of heated

HERE & NOW

BY THE TIME Bob and Irene started their left-wing magazine *Here & Now,* Bob had moved the Pelorus Press to 2A Severn Street, off Khyber Pass Road. In the first issue of October 1949, the original editorial panel consisted of Bob, A. R. D. Fairburn, Mary Dobbie, J. F. McDougall, M. K. Joseph, D. Knight Turner and Frank Hofmann. A 'Contributing Panel' included George Fraser, Kendrick Smithyman, David Ballantyne, Frank Sargeson, Maurice Duggan, Mervyn Taylor, Theo Schoon, Owen Jensen, Harold Baigent, Rae Griffiths and Helen Shaw. Irene was secretary and Frank Haigh the solicitor. Their aim was 'to ask all awkward questions, and speak out of turn as often as possible. We are sick of bureaucracy, whichever political party administers it, and dictatorship, however benevolent. We believe in that form of democracy in which free citizens mould their world a little nearer to their hearts' desire, through the full expression of opinion in a press as free as resolution can keep it from political or commercial control.' This last perhaps contributed to the fact that within a year, on 15 July 1950, a special meeting was called at the Lowrys' place to decide 'whether the publication of *Here & Now* should be resumed, and on what basis, financially and editorially, the magazine could operate in future'. The secretary reported that £427 10s of the required share capital was in hand, with £197 10s in the form of definite commitments. Nine hundred copies of the first issue had been sold, and 1200 of the second. The magazine, giving many artists and poets (and writers such as Sylvia Ashton-Warner) their first forum, was to last till November 1957 with issue 62.

Bob's sisters Iris and Jessie, aspiring author Jean Watson, I and my sisters (and our friends) were often called in to help at various of Bob's presses. Here began my habit of earning a bit (if lucky!) in school and varsity holidays, working as his bindery girl. It was my way of being close to him; otherwise I hardly saw him, except at weekends in his beloved vegetable garden. Printery assistant Robin Lush remembers a certain girl coming to him and saying 'Robin, do you want to hear a poem?' 'Yes,' he'd reply. 'Yum yum pig's bum makes good chewing gum!' and

ABOVE: THE PELORUS PRESS, 2A SEVERN ST, IN A FORMER BAKERY...
NOTE 'THE SPACE-EATER' WHICH BOB BOUGHT FROM NORAH DUMBLE.
BELOW: BOB'S HELPER ROBIN LUSH HARD AT WORK.

I'd run away, giggling. Working for my father could be fun, especially at lunchtimes when he would get one of us bindery hands to go out and buy a good feed. It would always consist of lettuce, cucumber, tomatoes, a crusty loaf with butter and a tin of smoked fish fillets or herrings in tomato sauce. We would gather in the bindery room and, after thoroughly washing his hands with Swarfega or pungent sandsoap, my father would entertain us all, printers, bindery hands, clients, visiting artists and poets, with his wit.

I remember one time towards the end when my father had a place in Airedale Street, and needed help to get out a university magazine that was running late. It was such a primitive shed there was no loo and we had to run over the road to our friends the Chrystalls, or squat down in the narrow space behind the shed! Architecture student David Mitchell was roped in to collect more students from O'Rorke Hall where he was living, which he was loath to do as they were in the middle of exams. I remember the tension of late-night sessions printing, folding, collating. I remember my father driving us in his little maroon van delivering helper Roger Horrocks home some time in the early morning, all of us speechless with exhaustion. But you couldn't *not* help my father, who could be extremely charming and persuasive when necessary.

Whichever press he was at, my father was kept very busy on jobbing work over the years — a huge variety, from concert and theatre programmes to slim volumes of verse and stories, literary magazines like *Pedagogue*, *Image* and *Mate*, wine labels, capping books, private ephemera such as the notice for the loo (which had a septic tank), raffle tickets, Tizard campaign leaflets, Kelston School report forms, Grand Prix account forms, stationery, business cards for Barry Crump, you name it! When offered a manuscript by Crump, though, Bob thought it 'bullshit' and rejected it on literary grounds. The manuscript was *A Good Keen Man* and would have made his fortune!

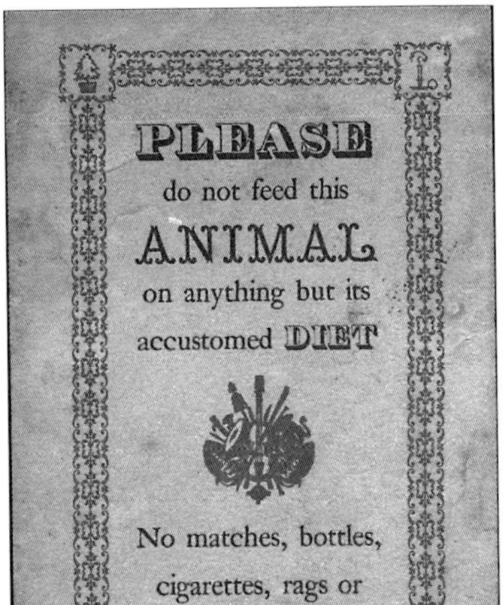

One of his most beautiful works was the children's book, *Biscotti and Caramelle*, with delightful illustrations by sculptor Molly Macalister. Bill Anso paid about £250 to have 1000 copies printed. The

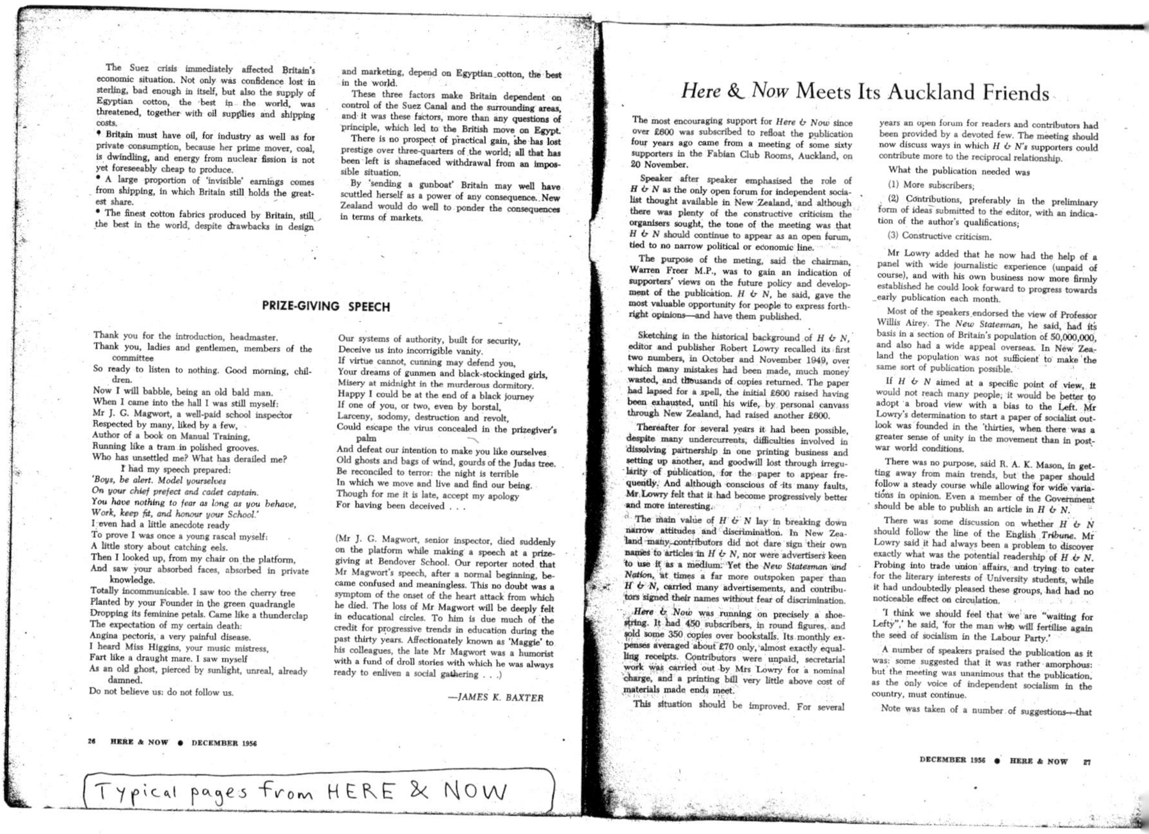

The Suez crisis immediately affected Britain's economic situation. Not only was confidence lost in sterling, bad enough in itself, but also the supply of Egyptian cotton, the best in the world, was threatened, together with oil supplies and shipping costs.

- Britain must have oil, for industry as well as for private consumption, because her prime mover, coal, is dwindling, and energy from nuclear fission is not yet foreseeably cheap to produce.
- A large proportion of 'invisible' earnings comes from shipping, in which Britain still holds the greatest share.
- The finest cotton fabrics produced by Britain, still the best in the world, despite drawbacks in design and marketing, depend on Egyptian cotton, the best in the world.

These three factors make Britain dependent on control of the Suez Canal and the surrounding areas, and it was these factors, more than any questions of principle, which led to the British move on Egypt.

There is no prospect of practical gain, she has lost prestige over three-quarters of the world; all that has been left is shamefaced withdrawal from an impossible situation.

By 'sending a gunboat' Britain may well have scuttled herself as a power of any consequence. New Zealand would do well to ponder the consequences in terms of markets.

PRIZE-GIVING SPEECH

Thank you for the introduction, headmaster.
Thank you, ladies and gentlemen, members of the committee
So ready to listen to nothing. Good morning, children.
Now I will babble, being an old bald man.
When I came into the hall I was still myself:
Mr J. G. Magwort, a well-paid school inspector
Respected by many, liked by a few,
Author of a book on Manual Training,
Running like a tram in polished grooves.
Who has unsettled me? What has derailed me?
I had my speech prepared:
'Boys, be alert. Model yourselves
On your chief prefect and cadet captain.
You have nothing to fear as long as you behave,
Work, keep fit, and honour your School.'
I even had a little anecdote ready
To prove I was once a young rascal myself:
A little story about catching eels.
Then I looked up, from my chair on the platform,
And saw your absorbed faces, absorbed in private knowledge.
Totally incommunicable. I saw too the cherry tree
Planted by your Founder in the green quadrangle
Dropping its feminine petals. Came like a thunderclap
The expectation of my certain death:
Angina pectoris, a very painful disease.
I heard Miss Higgins, your music mistress,
Fart like a draught mare. I saw myself
As an old ghost, pierced by sunlight, unreal, already damned.
Do not believe us: do not follow us.
Our systems of authority, built for security,
Deceive us into incorrigible vanity.
If virtue cannot, cunning may defend you,
Your dreams of gunmen and black-stockinged girls,
Misery at midnight in the murderous dormitory.
Happy I could be at the end of a black journey
If one of you, or two, even by borstal,
Larceny, sodomy, destruction and revolt,
Could escape the virus concealed in the prizegiver's palm
And defeat our intention to make you like ourselves
Old ghosts and bags of wind, gourds of the Judas tree.
Be reconciled to terror: the night is terrible
In which we move and live and find our being.
Though for me it is late, accept my apology
For having been deceived . . .

(Mr J. G. Magwort, senior inspector, died suddenly on the platform while making a speech at a prize-giving at Bendover School. Our reporter noted that Mr Magwort's speech, after a normal beginning, became confused and meaningless. This no doubt was a symptom of the onset of the heart attack from which he died. The loss of Mr Magwort will be deeply felt in educational circles. To him is due much of the credit for progressive trends in education during the past thirty years. Affectionately known as 'Maggie' to his colleagues, the late Mr Magwort was a humorist with a fund of droll stories with which he was always ready to enliven a social gathering . . .)

—*JAMES K. BAXTER*

26 HERE & NOW • DECEMBER 1956

Here & Now Meets Its Auckland Friends

The most encouraging support for *Here & Now* since over £600 was subscribed to refloat the publication four years ago came from a meeting of some sixty supporters in the Fabian Club Rooms, Auckland, on 20 November.

Speaker after speaker emphasised the role of *H & N* as the only open forum for independent socialist thought available in New Zealand, and although there was plenty of the constructive criticism the organisers sought, the tone of the meeting was that *H & N* should continue to appear as an open forum, tied to no narrow political or economic line.

The purpose of the meting, said the chairman, Warren Freer M.P., was to gain an indication of supporters' views on the future policy and development of the publication. *H & N*, he said, gave the most valuable opportunity for people to express forthright opinions—and have them published.

Sketching in the historical background of *H & N*, editor and publisher Robert Lowry recalled its first two numbers, in October and November 1949, over which many mistakes had been made, much money wasted, and thousands of copies returned. The paper had lapsed for a spell, the initial £600 raised having been exhausted, until his wife, by personal canvass through New Zealand, had raised another £600.

Thereafter for several years it had been possible, despite many undercurrents, difficulties involved in dissolving partnership in one printing business and setting up another, and goodwill lost through irregularity of publication, for the paper to appear frequently. And although conscious of its many faults, Mr Lowry felt that it had become progressively better and more interesting.

The main value of *H & N* lay in breaking down narrow attitudes and discrimination. In New Zealand many contributors did not dare sign their own names to articles in *H & N*, nor were advertisers keen to use it as a medium. Yet the *New Statesman and Nation*, at times a far more outspoken paper than *H & N*, carried many advertisements, and contributors signed their names without fear of discrimination.

Here & Now was running on precisely a shoestring. It had 450 subscribers, in round figures, and sold some 350 copies over bookstalls. Its monthly expenses averaged about £70 only, almost exactly equalling receipts. Contributors were unpaid, secretarial work was carried out by Mrs Lowry for a nominal charge, and a printing bill very little above cost of materials made ends meet.

This situation should be improved. For several years an open forum for readers and contributors had been provided by a devoted few. The meeting should now discuss ways in which *H & N's* supporters could contribute more to the reciprocal relationship.

What the publication needed was

(1) More subscribers;

(2) Contributions, preferably in the preliminary form of ideas submitted to the editor, with an indication of the author's qualifications;

(3) Constructive criticism.

Mr Lowry added that he now had the help of a panel with wide journalistic experience (unpaid of course), and with his own business now more firmly established he could look forward to progress towards early publication each month.

Most of the speakers endorsed the view of Professor Willis Airey. The *New Statesman*, he said, had its basis in a section of Britain's population of 50,000,000, and also had a wide appeal overseas. In New Zealand the population was not sufficient to make the same sort of publication possible.

If *H & N* aimed at a specific point of view, it would not reach many people; it would be better to adopt a broad view with a bias to the Left. Mr Lowry's determination to start a paper of socialist outlook was founded in the 'thirties, when there was a greater sense of unity in the movement than in post-war world conditions.

There was no purpose, said R. A. K. Mason, in getting away from main trends, but the paper should follow a steady course while allowing for wide variations in opinion. Even a member of the Government should be able to publish an article in *H & N*.

There was some discussion on whether *H & N* should follow the line of the English *Tribune*. Mr Lowry said it had always been a problem to discover exactly what was the potential readership of *H & N*. Probing into trade union affairs, and trying to cater for the literary interests of University students, while it had undoubtedly pleased these groups, had had no noticeable effect on circulation.

'I think we should feel that we are "waiting for Lefty",' he said, 'for the man who will fertilise again the seed of socialism in the Labour Party.'

A number of speakers praised the publication as it was: some suggested that it was rather amorphous: but the meeting was unanimous that the publication, as the only voice of independent socialism in the country, must continue.

Note was taken of a number of suggestions—that

DECEMBER 1956 • HERE & NOW 27

Typical pages from HERE & NOW

copyright was made out to me as the boy Biscotti and Carolyn Dobbie as Caramelle, but all the Dobbie and Lowry girls, as well as Bill's daughters Daphne and Tina (who later married Crump and bore him two little 'Crumpets'), were used as inspiration. Bill Anso recalled in a letter to me: 'One summer morning early, Bob arrived home with a dislocated shoulder, broken arm and collar-bone, from a spill in loose gravel on his motor-bike, called the Space-Eater. Irene met him, and only I was there. All of you [girls] had gone to school. Her concern and care were good to see, and her love shone in her eyes for her Bob. He called her "Toots" and I think there is a song about that, "In The Good Old Summertime".' Another memory Bill called 'The Miracle of the Loaves and Fishes':

> A large pot was filled with potatoes, washed and with their skins on, and a few sprigs of mint and a bit of salt. This was boiled and half eaten for supper with some meat, sausage and bacon and butter with cabbage, or fish, and tea or coffee. A jolly meal, all happy and talking together. The next morning the half-pot of cold potatoes were peeled, cut into "dollars" and fried in butter or olive oil. And often a black pudding cut into dollars and fried too, with a bit of bacon. Good! Then everybody went off about their business and worked like Trojans — for Troy had to be built and there were great hopes for it. That it was destroyed by a wooden horse was unfortunate, later ...

Bob's motorbike featured also in one of his mother-in-law's memories. Bob and Denis Glover once arrived by motorbike at the Wade property after midnight in a state of intoxication, making such a din that Gran erupted from the Cornes' bach clad only in white nightie and sandshoes, and ordered them off the property. It was Irene who smoothed things over as usual. Gran, who mellowed as she neared 101, would laugh about it whenever she heard the famous poet Glover on the radio. Judy remembered one time at the Wade: 'Pop built a cold shower onto one side of the new bach. When Gran was taking a shower one day a friend of Dad's came around the corner to take a leak and he saw her. Both were pretty embarrassed but the friend just joked, "Oh, I'm sorry, Mrs Cornes, I thought you were a tea-tree bush!" Even dry old Gran thought it was funny, I think.'

Here & Now had several editors, all of whom (as Bob wrote in the editorial of December 1955) 'have had real and sufficient reason to be chary of identifying themselves ... present editor is Robert Lowry, who is also the publisher of the paper. Punch-drunk with advancing years, he now commits his identity to the Security Division, his fingerprints to the Americans, his blood to Mr Holland's police dogs, his soul to the Archbishop of Canterbury, his body to the Rhinemaidens, his footprints to time's trackless sands. And tallyho the fox!' In a footnote to this editorial he notes the secretary's suggestion that 'the editor of the *Listener* is probably a squid, because he discharges inky clouds when he's attacked. And whenever he opens his mouth he puts his footnote in it.'

Malayan Fish Dish

1 lb fish
2 ozs butter
2 ozs flour
2 teasp. curry pdr
2 " chutney
3 slices pineapple, finely chopped.
Milk
½ cup cooked rice
Salt & pepper
2 hard-boiled eggs, sliced to garnish.

Poach fish in a little water – barely cook. Take out bones & flake. Keep juice.
Melt butter, stir in flour, add curry, chutney & pineapple.
Gradually stir in fish juice, with enough milk to make 1 pint. Stir till boiling.
Add fish, rice, salt & pepper, and a little lemon juice (or vinegar).
Garnish with egg slices.

IRENE'S

FISH FILLETS in Cream

Judy's

1 kilo fish fillets

1 250 ml. bottle of cream

a handful of scallops

a handful of mushrooms

cayenne pepper to taste (a pinch)

parmesan cheese / salt.

Lay fish in flat casserole.
Arrange scallops evenly on top.
Put mushrooms (round side up) over this
Sprinkle cayenne & salt on top, then cream.
Put into oven - moderate heat - for 15 mins - 20 mins
Take out. Scatter parmesan over and grill 5 mins.

Lowry girls continue party tradition

Party for Janet Dumble (crouching centre)

MY FATHER WAS spending more and more time in the pubs, to the detriment of his work and family life. English sculptor Tony Stones remembers those days. He first met Bob in the Queen's Ferry, along with Kevin Ireland, Carl Freeman, and Fassett Burnett, who took him there. Tony was only twenty, but there was no distinction about age. If it was decided, or other people just assumed, that you had talent and were serious, they took you at that value. Tony was then busy illustrating John Yelash's book of 'spell-binding stories, *Forty Thousand Beers Ago*. It was really neat being involved with Bob and the printing. Bob was helluva good at planning the stuff and laying it out, and designing. He had a terrific instinct for what was right, or not so much that as the inspired recycling of what he'd got.'

Tony remembers some amazing parties at One Tree Hill. There'd be a great range of people, 'from Members of Parliament and university professors and arts people to drunken young buggers like me'. He remembers Irene had a strange way of speaking, perhaps a family accent, unlike a New Zealand accent. 'She was neat, sort of laconic, with a marvellously dry style which was just what was needed for Bob, as he was so burbly and Rabelaisian and bubbly.' The night before Jim Baxter went to India they were sitting around the big kauri table in the kitchen, Jim telling stories, Bob at the head of the table. Bob used to get a bit annoyed with Jim and 'would say that he did all this sinning on purpose so that he could feel guilty and go through all this religious performance. Bob was a good critic, for he said what he meant, and thought, and his judgement was pretty good, particularly in matters of design and illustration. He had a sort of instinct for the right typeface, just the — ping! — right layout.' Tony remembers Bob as a brilliant talker, one with marvellously anarchical opinions but who managed to make it all so light-hearted. 'One or two people were a bit heavy and gloomy about things, but Bob was a person who illuminated life, shone his light into corners and made it all look good.'

ABOVE: TRAINING COLLEGE BALL '62; VANYA & TERRY HUNTER, RIGHT

TEACHER: MISS JEWEL. VANYA THIRD ROW, FIFTH FROM RIGHT.

IRENE & BOB WITH JUDY AT HER MARRIAGE TO DAVID MITCHELL

The Lowry Family
which in its heyday fondly imagined itself
to be provided with an almost unlimited supply
of marriageable wenches
finds late in 1961 that various young beatniks
are scraping the bottom of its barrel.
This notwithstanding, it wishes all its readers
a Merry Christmas and a Happy New Year.

The Lowry Family says to Hell with Holyoake anyhow
—he only proves that a little bull goes a long way.

INVITATION TO THE WAYZGOOSE

★

Robert Lowry, Robin Lush and Jean Watson request the pleasure of your company at a brief impromptu and informal exhibition of painting, typography, hospitality and objets d'art, to be held at The Pilgrim Press, in the basement of Ashington House, 75 Wakefield St, on Friday 21 December from 1 p.m. to 6.

Wayzgoose, n. Printing-house's annual festivity. [earlier *waygoose* (1683; *wayz-* 1731), etym. dub.]
The Concise Oxford Dictionary

Star [illegible] 26 [illegible] 1959

Small printery wins recognition again

For the second time in three years the Auckland typographer Robert Lowry has won international recognition for his Pilgrim Press.

The recognition was shared with the University of Auckland's bindery, for the production and design of the bibliography "A. R. D. Fairburn, 1904-1957," compiled by Miss Olive Johnson, of the University Library.

This was one of ten New Zealand books selected primarily for good design for the International Book Design Exhibition which will open in London next May. After the London exhibition the books will be circulated in the United Kingdom and other countries.

The Pilgrim Press also won a place in the same exhibition in 1957 with Maurice Duggan's "Immanuel's Land," a collection of short stories, the design and printing of which were carried out by Mr Lowry and the binding by the Disabled Servicemen's Re-Establishment League.

Over a period of many years Mr Lowry has been associated with the production of typographically outstanding New Zealand publications, ranging from volumes of verse and short stories to light-hearted efforts like Fairburn's chaotic "How to Ride a Bicycle in Seventeen Lovely Colours."

Let writers rage, let poets rant in rhymes,
The printer Lowry takes his fucking time.

attributed to D.G.

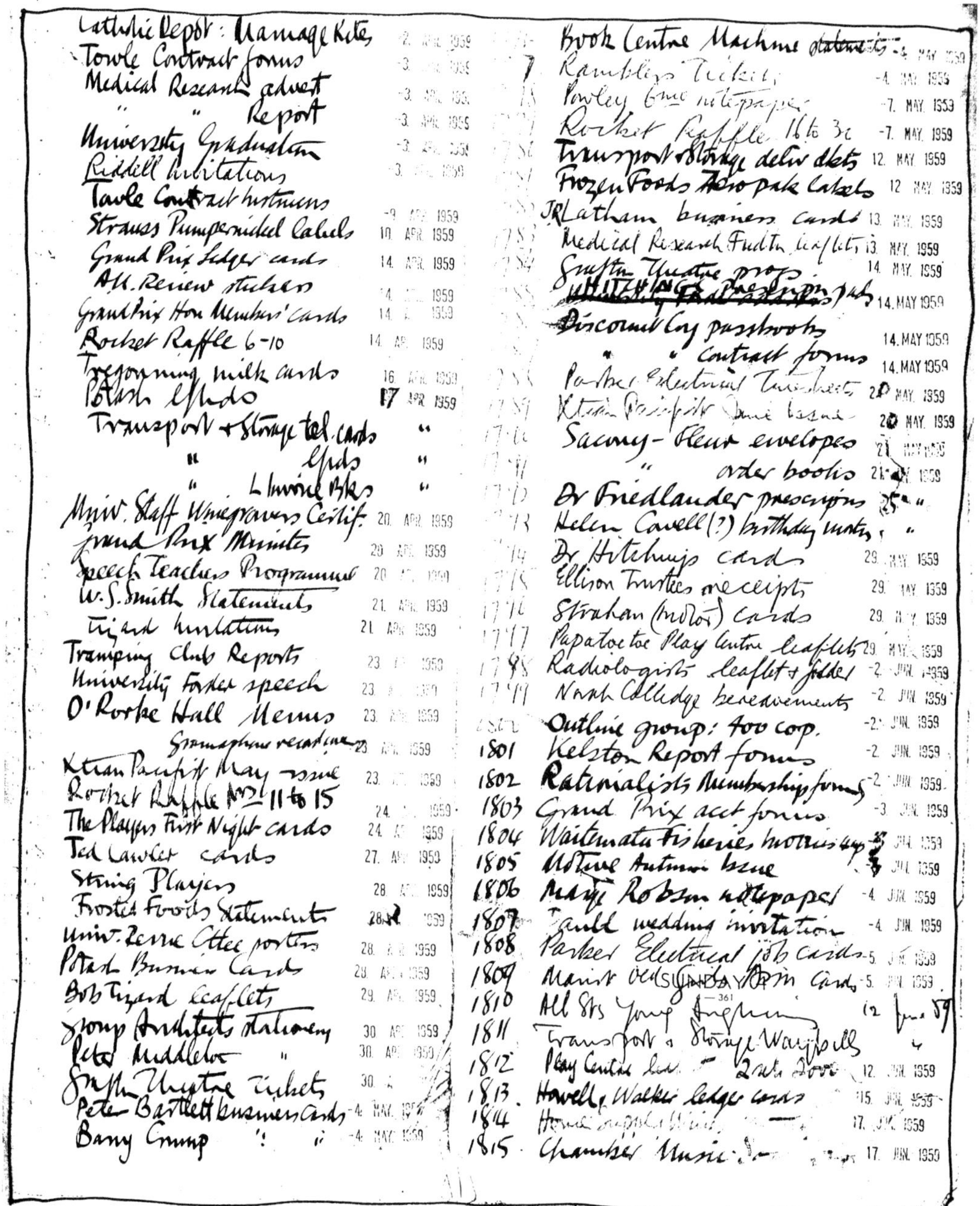
Catholic Depot: Marriage Kits	2 APR 1959
Towle Contract forms	3 APR 1959
Medical Research advert	3 APR 1959
" " Report	3 APR 1959
University Graduation	3 APR 1959
Riddell Invitations	3 APR 1959
Towle Contract instruments	
Strauss Pumpernickel Labels	9 APR 1959 / 10 APR 1959
Grand Prix Ledger cards	14 APR 1959
All. Review stickers	14 APR 1959
Grand Prix Hon Members' cards	14 APR 1959
Rocket Raffle 6–10	14 APR 1959
Tregonning milk cards	16 APR 1959
Potash Efrods	17 APR 1959
Transport + Storage tel. cards	"
" Gpds	"
" L Invoice Bks	"
Univ. Staff Wine-growers Certif.	20 APR 1959
Grand Prix Minutes	20 APR 1959
Speech Teachers Programmes	20 APR 1959
W. S. Smith Statements	21 APR 1959
Tizard Invitations	21 APR 1959
Tramping Club Reports	23 APR 1959
University Forker speech	23 APR 1959
O'Rorke Hall Menus	23 APR 1959
Gramophone recordings	23 APR 1959
Xtian Pacifist May issue	23 APR 1959
Rocket Raffle Nos 11 to 15	24 APR 1959
The Players First Night cards	24 APR 1959
Ted Lawler cards	27 APR 1959
String Players	28 APR 1959
Frosted Foods Statements	28 APR 1959
Univ. Reserve Cttee posters	28 APR 1959
Potash Business Cards	28 APR 1959
Bob Tizard leaflets	29 APR 1959
Group Architects stationery	30 APR 1959
Peter Middleton "	30 APR 1959
Griffin Theatre tickets	30 APR 1959
Peter Bartlett business cards	4 MAY 1959
Barry Crump " "	4 MAY 1959

	Book Centre Machine statements	4 MAY 1959
	Ramblers Tickets	4 MAY 1959
	Rowley 6 nil notepaper	7 MAY 1959
	Rocket Raffle 16 to 32	7 MAY 1959
	Transport & Storage deliv dkts	12 MAY 1959
	Frozen Foods Aeropak Labels	12 MAY 1959
	JR Latham business cards	13 MAY 1959
	Medical Research Fund leaflets	13 MAY 1959
	Griffin Theatre progs	14 MAY 1959
	Discount Coy passbooks	14 MAY 1959
	" " contract forms	14 MAY 1959
	Parker Electrical timesheets	14 MAY 1959
	Xtian Pacifist June issue	20 MAY 1959
	Sacony-Fleur envelopes	20 MAY 1959
	" order books	21 MAY 1959
	Dr Friedlander prescriptions	25 "
	Helen Cavell (?) birthday invites	"
	Dr Hitchings cards	29 MAY 1959
	Ellison Trustees receipts	29 MAY 1959
	Strahan (Motor) cards	29 MAY 1959
	Papatoetoe Play Centre leaflets	29 MAY 1959
	Radiologists leaflet + folder	2 JUN 1959
	North College bereavements	2 JUN 1959
	Outline group: 400 cop.	2 JUN 1959
1801	Kelston Report forms	2 JUN 1959
1802	Rationalists Membership forms	2 JUN 1959
1803	Grand Prix acct forms	3 JUN 1959
1804	Waitemata Fisheries invoices	3 JUN 1959
1805	Motive Autumn Issue	3 JUN 1959
1806	Marge Robson notepaper	4 JUN 1959
1807	Cahill wedding invitation	4 JUN 1959
1808	Parker Electrical job cards	5 JUN 1959
1809	Marist Old Boys Assn cards	5 JUN 1959
1810	All Sts Young Anglicans	12 June 59
1811	Transport & Storage Waybills	4
1812	Play Centre leaflets – 2 wks 2000	12 JUN 1959
1813	Howell & Walker ledger cards	15 JUN 1959
1814	Home Supplies	17 JUN 1959
1815	Chamber Music	17 JUN 1959

A typical page from Bob's Jobbing Book

In 1953 Bob had left the Pelorus Press after falling out with partners Gordon Trigg and Les Taylor, and in 1954 established the Pilgrim Press at 75 Wakefield Street, just over the road from the Globe Hotel. One time when I was about fifteen he parked the van on the slope beside the press and left me sitting in the passenger seat as he started across the road to the Globe for urgent refreshment. Unfortunately, he hadn't put the brake on properly, so I sat there, too terrified to yell for help, as the van began to roll down the slope. Fortunately, he looked back and, running, managed to get back in to jam on the brake. After this he made sure I knew the rudiments of driving (though I never did get my driver's licence).

By 1959 Pilgrim was in trouble, and in August 'was incorporated with two partners providing new capital, but in February 1961 the company could not meet loan repayments and went into receivership', being taken over as the

Wakefield Press, as Peter Hughes notes in his entry in the *Dictionary of New Zealand Biography, Volume 4*. Bob returned to work for Wakefield in 1962 as 'resident typographer' and composed a whimsical little book of typefaces and clever printing exercises ('Try a beard, man, it grows on you!') before leaving to work from the office of Group Architects, where I assisted him as 'gofer' in the 1963 May holidays. He worked briefly for Whitcombe & Tombs, then as a proofreader at the *Auckland Star*.

EARLY IN 1963 MY father gave a well-attended lecture to senior students at Elam School of Fine Arts, where I was by now enrolled. In May he and I attended the Arts Ball at the Peter Pan Cabaret. I was Gertrude Stein and he was the One-Eyed King (Farouk), with a fake McCahon that I'd painted pinned to the chest of his (hired) kingly robes. One of the judges was Hamish Keith, and Bob won a prize for the Most Original Costume.

King Farouk & Gertrude Stein - Firth's Studio

THE OPUSCULE
"THE OPUSCULE"
WAR!
Dellow . U.S.A.
2nd. CADET BATTN. SAILS
The McBrausch-stead Way
And now we are on the eve of discovering our 4th. and greatest Aid.
SEE NEXT ISSUE.
THE PHOENIX
VALLEY OF DECISION
Poems by Allen Curnow
HOUSE TO HOUSE
AUCKLAND UNIVERSITY COLLEGE
LABOUR CLUB 1937
PEACE, FREEDOM AND PROGRESS
KIVVI:
AVCKLAND
MDCCCCXXXII
Katherine Mansfield
this book is
robin lowry's
a little book
with insects
a little book
with
insects in it
KIWI
Major Axis defeat in Tunisia
ENEMY FLUNG BACK 75 MILES
Heavy enemy losses
Rocco the Rooster

Bob's 1963 exhibition at Elam School of Fine Arts

On 13 May 1963 my father's Retrospective was mounted at Elam School of Fine Arts, as part of an exhibition 'Designed in New Zealand', for the 15th Auckland Festival. Opening the show, Dr W. B. Sutch commented on the catalogue which my father had designed for editor Des Mahoney:

> Auckland is to be congratulated on the catalogue for the Design Festival. Not only is it an excellent guide to what is on each day, it is an admirably produced piece of typography. When we realise how difficult it is to incorporate advertisements in a brochure of this kind, it becomes all the more evident what a good job Bob Lowry has made of the production. In some cases, of course, the symbols and other designs used by the advertisers have prevented a completely unified job. New Zealand is fortunate in having a few typographers who have refused to compromise with triviality, and Mr Lowry is one of this small number .... If one turns to the examples in this exhibition of the typographical art in New Zealand, one sees ... A high quality job perhaps somewhat less solemn in some cases. There are some good examples of typography from several printers but I would particularly draw your attention to the kind of work shown here from one of your Auckland typographers, Robert Lowry. New Zealand is fortunate to have him. We should cherish our Bob Lowrys.

But in my journal I wrote:

> My father is dying. I have found a name for his disease. I shall call it cancer of the soul which begins by taking your soul and throwing it down from some unimaginable high moon to form a tiny bruise, a bruise that spreads through your flesh and is transmitted to everything that flesh touches, including the flesh of others, till it becomes a great purple bleeding sadness. So, we are leaving him, taking all our things from this house where our nights have become loud with ogres and our days only pauses between each black night. We are leaving him now and he is alone. His eyes no longer see except the vision of his death which I fear will come soon. I return to show him how to use the washing-machine, for I have seen him going to give a lecture at the

Artschool with foodstains down his jersey. The house is dead too, the windows blank eyes. My baby has begun to stir in me. I have forgotten the touch of any man. The child and I are strong in each other. Now, the world of my father and of our home is become nothing, now we have left him. Though I love and regret both of them dearly it is too late.

ABOVE: BOB AT AIREDALE STREET

WHAT'S LEFT OF THE LOWRY FAMILY
IS SHOWN HERE WITHDRAWING ITS OFFENSIVE WEAPONS
TWELVE MILES BEYOND THE POINT OF CONTROL.
FEELING EXTRA PEACEFULLY COEXISTENT THIS CHRISTMAS
IT CAN'T EVEN BE BOTHERED TO MAKE IT S USUAL JIBE
AT THE NATIONAL PARTY.
JUST LET'S ALL HAVE A WHALE OF A GOOD TIME.

★

IRENE, ROBERT, VANYA & BRIGID LOWRY : 32 GLADWIN RD, AUCKLAND S.E.3
ROBIN, ROGER, RACHEL & DAVID HAY : 27 LITHGOW ST, INVERCARGILL
JUDITH & DAVID MITCHELL : 118 ST STEPHENS AVE, AUCKLAND C.4

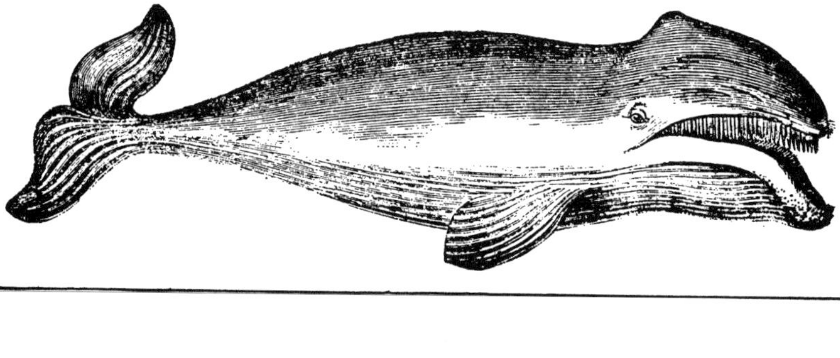

PART THREE: ENDINGS

But at my back I alwaies hear
Time's winged charriot hurrying near;

ANDREW MARVELL : *To My Coy Mistress*

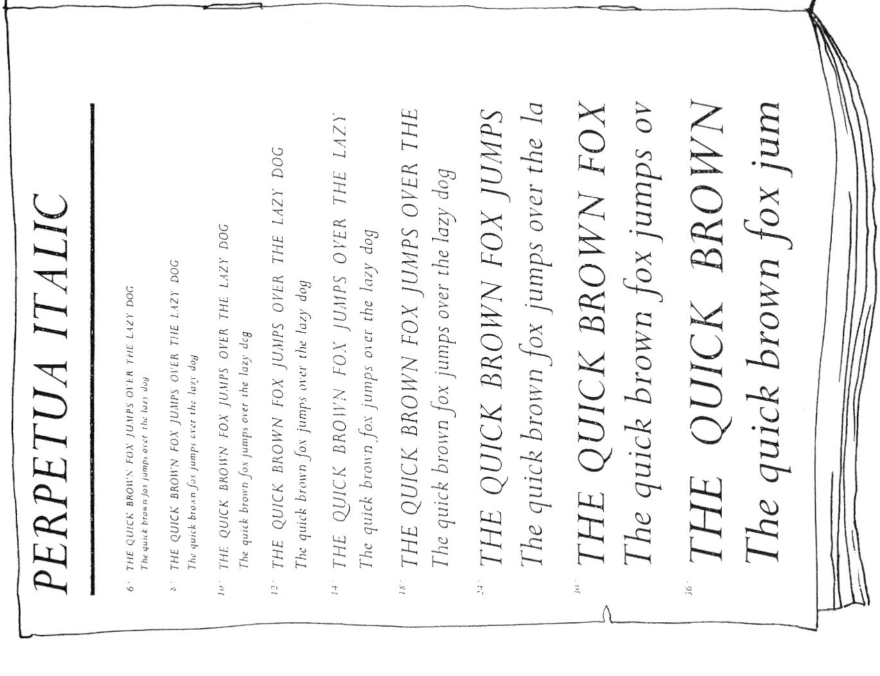

IRENE & VANYA

ON 7 DECEMBER 1963, my father ended it. One of the drifters staying in the One Tree Hill house took him a cup of tea in the morning, and found Bob in the armchair in his study with a water jug and glass and the five bottles of sleeping pills he'd saved, empty. At the last minute he'd scrawled a note saying 'Forgive me'. But how can we forgive death, how can death decide who is right and who is wrong? Our father had so many friends who wanted to help him but, because of his pride and volatile temper and alcoholic unpredictability, were unable to. He left no will, nothing but debts and sad memories. With a refund of my art school fees (kindly arranged by friends at the law school where my mother was a valued staff member) we were able to pay £80 for a returned serviceman's burial. Though my father had always said he wanted cremation, we could not afford the extra cost. I have always deeply regretted this, and wish I could put it right so that his spirit could rest in peace.

How could we have let this happen to him? Did he know how all of us left behind would suffer for the rest of our lives because we had not known how to help him then? I suspect he had been depressed for a long time, ever since the death from kidney cancer of his eldest grand-daughter, Kirsten Hay, not yet three years old. At One Tree Hill after her funeral was the only time I saw my father cry; and it shocked me to see it. After that he was bereft when Robin moved south with her husband, Roger Hay, for he missed Robin and their love-hate relationship; as he said to friend Don McRae, 'Why did he have to take her to Invercargill? It may as well be to Antarctica.' Then, with the diagnosis of his liver cirrhosis, he could not face a slow decline; he'd always vowed he would not be a burden to anyone in old age. Also, he could not face a life without alcohol.

Dr M gave him 'uppers' that did not help, and in fact exacerbated the high cycle of his manic depression. Could we not have got him committed to a psychiatric hospital for treatment, or at least to see a counsellor? But in those days men were not expected to suffer nervous breakdowns, they just became alcoholics instead. But with his business affairs again in tatters, and his health deteriorating, my father's behaviour became so erratic that we (my mother, sister Brigid and I) were scared to stay at One Tree Hill with him. In November we had no choice but to move out, staying in the attic belonging to Judy and her husband, David Mitchell, at 54 Hepburn Street in Freemans Bay. I believe that is when our father began saving the sleeping pills the doctor had prescribed to counter the 'speed'. I remember the last time I saw him, 17 November, when he had come over to the Mitchells' house for dinner to celebrate his fifty-first birthday. Though I could ill afford it, I had bought him a present, a collection of Bertrand Russell in Penguin. He barely glanced at it. Heaven knows what we had to eat or drink. All I remember is the sadness, for my father was in complete defeat and could barely lift his head to speak. I told him I would come back to the house one day soon to collect my pushbike from the shed. But I put off doing it.

And a few weeks later, when my little sister and I awoke in the Hepburn Street attic room we shared, our mother in the adjoining room was standing with a distraught Dr M at the top of the stairs. She was murmuring that 'the girls will have to know sooner or later, they might as well hear it now'. Brigid's arms were around my swelling waist as we clung together in the doorway, fearful of what the dreadful news would be. Dr M said that our father had died of an overdose.

In all the distress and activity of the next few days, the fact that I'd passed all my first-year exams in Fine Arts went almost unnoticed, except for my childhood friend Carolyn ('Caramelle' to my 'Biscotti') who sent me a congratulatory bunch of lovely red roses. She must have forgiven me for that time long ago when I had got hacked off with her bossing me about and took a good bite out of her arm. The worst thing was, there was no floor in the Mitchells' kitchen, as our architect brother-in-law had just removed all the rotten floorboards, which somehow seemed symbolic. Now with some friends' help David had to work frantically night and day to get a new floor in before our father's wake at Hepburn Street that weekend. At which I was so stunned I can remember absolutely nothing . . .

George Gunn vividly remembered the burial on the Waikumete hillside that fine Tuesday afternoon, 10 December 1963. 'There was, of course, a huge crowd there, amongst them some of the country's most interesting people . . . Denis Glover delivered the panegyric, obviously after some "divine libations". There he stood, or rather swayed, by the mouth of the open grave, looking as if at any minute he would join his late friend in a common grave. It was a very moving occasion and a fitting farewell to a great member of the human race whom I was privileged to know.'

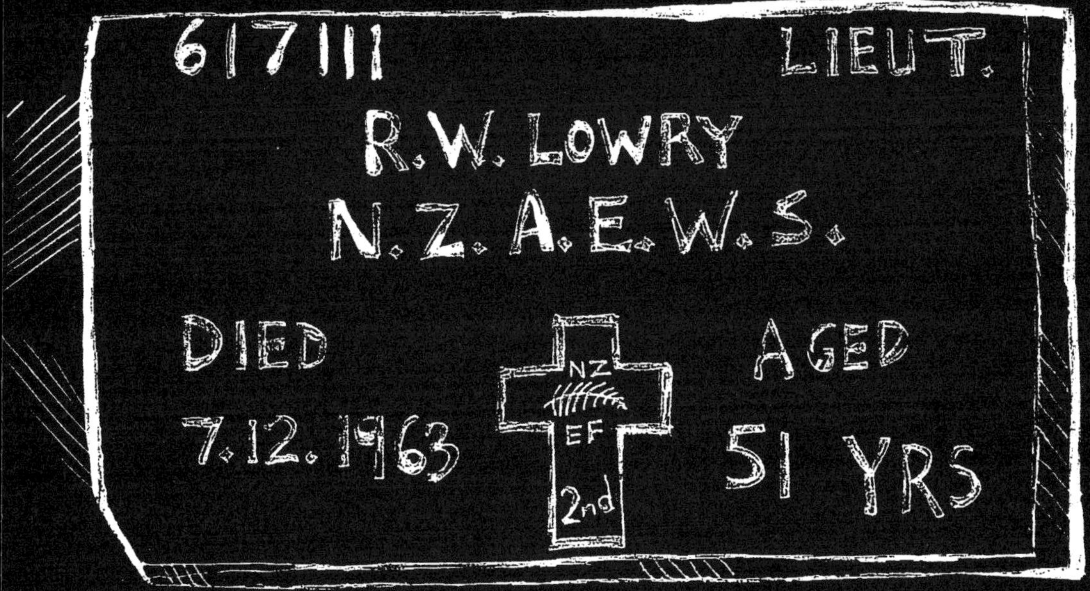

Jean Bartlett, an early flame of Bob's, remembered that 'Glover said "This is the worst day of my life" and burst into tears . . .'

My sister Judy vividly remembers it as well; she went prematurely into labour with her eldest, Benjamin Robert!

In my journal I wrote:

> It is hot and bright on this hillside. Voluptuous cloudwomen lie easily at the melting rim of this vast and creamy sky above my father's grave. Round the coffin spill great petalled heaps of flowers. Here remorsefully on this hillside we stand grouped and still, waiting for him to come so we can begin. All of us who were once his friends, those who loved him and those he loved, those who betrayed him, who destroyed him for he needed so much love. And so we wait. But already the gnomes of death have robbed him of his good blood, the five pill bottles are empty. And the lumps of dry earth close over him for he will not come . . .

Tribute paid to a fine N. Zealand typographer

TO be an artist or expert in any field does necessarily cut a man off from a great deal of what goes on around him. Bob Lowry, I think, was somebody who contained the whole universe within the eggshell of his own skull.

Many of us feel this, but many realize all of a sudden that there is a world to which we are responsible. Bob always thought the world was his—he was there to do what he thought important with single-minded purpose, ruthlessly, remorselessly, sometimes erratically and often unpunctually. He was answerable only to the brilliant thoughts in his own mind.

I first met Bob when we were both 14 and I came as a freckle - nosed schoolboy to Auckland Grammar. We made an immediate friendship, and nothing since has undermined my love for and faith in Bob Lowry.

We founded an informal magazine which got us both into trouble. Bob then got hold of the notion of using printing types, and I followed in his footsteps.

Devotion

Both of us were up against a complete lack of good type, and had no knowledge of how to work printing machinery. Bob had an impassioned devotion to getting the impossible done; he did it.

Bob was not concerned, as I became later, with what they were doing in England or on the Continent. Where I was a typographical purist, regarding printing as a disciplined job, the handmaiden of literature, Bob would take any piece of printing and translate it into a miraculous piece of creative genius.

Type talked

Many people can be good typographers. It is a matter of discipline. Bob was undisiplined, but he would make type talk, any type. The trouble he would go to over the most trifling things, even if they were delivered a week late was extraordinary.

When he found Rex Fairburn it was clear that here was a combination of fantastic Rabelaisian humour. Rex would fire off the ideas, Bob translate them into type. The world is a silly mad place, full of mortgages and monkeys, and the wrong Government is always in. Bob would press on with the thought: "Is humour worth having? If I can do it, let them have it."

When he wanted to be a serious typographer, apart from playing round with exotic ideas and types, he proved himself intensely capable of disciplining himself to the requirements of the audience which he addressed. It was done with unmistakable genius; anyone who knew type would say: "I'll bet Bob did that."

What he actually did is not nearly as important as the fact that he existed. His influence on other people, on typography and printing and his joy of living were the things for which many hundreds of us will always be grateful.

Robert W. Lowry, who died last week at the early age of 51, was the father of modern typography in New Zealand. With DENIS GLOVER, who contributes this appreciation, he worked from an early age to raise the standard of typography and printing here, and many of the finest and most arresting publications of the last 30 years had come from his hands. His last major creations were the much-praised Auckland Festival Society programme this year and the papers of the architectural Pacific Congress.

"Auckland Star"

Ironically, Bob Lowry was to become almost as well known by the poems written about him after his death as for his actual work. Take, for example, Jim Baxter's 'Ballad of One Tree Hill', which begins:

Old friend, let us converse
Again a little — at a table in the Queen's Ferry
Let it be — brandy for you,
Tonic water for me, while the afternoon ripens like a plum . . .

(Jim never persuaded Bob to join him in Alcoholics Anonymous.) The ballad ends:

High above One Tree Hill
Like a skull rose up the moon,
And the town opened her thighs
To let sorrow in;

At the Globe in Wakefield Street
One barman told another
That Lowry had lain down with
The hyena-headed mother.

The grass grows long at Waikumete,
The ink has dried on the printing stone.
Take no notice, Bob;
All things burn.

Or 'Auckland':

Anno Domini 1956

Here Lowry lived, a stone volcanic god
Fed with honey and red gourds,
Opening his heart like a great door
To poets, lovers, and the houseless poor.

As Denis Glover had poetically written in *Book* 8: 'There is no delicate innuendo about Auckland, or Aucklanders. Virtue is not modest, not in Auckland. It runs to ten-foot hoardings in front of churches. And so typography, in the hands of an Aucklander, becomes not so much the ubiquitous willow, resourceful yet yielding, useful but still graceful, but rather a pohutukawa in riotous raging blossom.'

And Mike Jackson in 'Remembering the Wade':

> I brought her here five years after
> you were dead, to the bach and estuary.
> We lay back in the carved bunk
> with the black wind of night knocking
> at the pines while over the far land
> rain sped towards us and I heard
> your ghost rummaging in the small hours
> for a bottle, in the kitchen, or
> stacking manuka branches by the stove
> for us to burn.

And from Kendrick Smithyman's 'Grotesques':

> So much sustained you, so much you sustained
> When you laid words to words and botched a page.
> Not that you could not do it otherwise
> (You could and easily) but that you would,
> Throwing the city up against your will.
> You lived in symbols till your symptoms stank.
> Who were the boys who stoned your windows out?
> You kept an open house, but when the glass
> Was done the night came in. That night was long.

Many kind people wrote letters. Terry Bond wrote to my mother that:

> The basis of Bob's tragedy was that he had capacities that went far beyond the demands or appreciations of New Zealanders generally, but

> in a larger environment he would have found outlets and ... supporters who would have borne with his faults, and he would have been saved from the spiritual despair that overtakes those so constantly frustrated. In the latter years he must have been very difficult to live with and you must have had much to cope with ... Most of us will remember him for his wit and grand sense of fun, for his good natured and often acute perception and his very real gifts and achievements. Memory of those and of the better years you had together must be of some help to you now ...

And from Joan Harrow:

> My dear Irene,
> Ken and I were shocked and saddened to learn of Bob's sudden death & do wish you to accept our deepest sympathy & our kindest loving thoughts for you & the children just now. You've done so much over all the years — you've always been my absolute definition of that old-fashioned word helpmeet & if there is anything at all that we can do for you please let us help you now.

And Jim Baxter:

> Dearest Irene,
> I heard today that Bob is dead. That is very very tough: No doubt a great many people beside myself loved Bob, for he had an open heart to many. Last time I was in Auckland I spent some time with him. I know he was worried about the separation, but deep down knew you had shifted for his good as well as your own, and that you still loved him. I hope you had no regrets whatsoever — the relation between the two of you was one of the best things I have ever seen in any marriage — and all the difficulties Bob got into never really shovelled dirt over that. I don't claim to know much about you and Bob — I just camped in the shade of the wall sometimes — but I would have to have been blind not to see there was something entirely magnificent in what you were to one another, underneath every difficulty. Please accept my fondest love and blessings ...

In May 1964, after *Craccum* student newspaper was censored for obscene language, Baxter wrote in a subsequent *Craccum*:

> I remember Bob Lowry, that Aucklander who loved his fellows greatly, and loved the arts most whenever they were most human — a man who rarely spoke without using a four-letter word — I remember him walking round Auckland University with me pointing out corners and balconies where he and his girlfriend used to cohabit when both were students. If a poem could have been written about the great rabbit-warren on the hill, he would have been the man to write it; for he lived without social ambition, without money, not concerned with the big names and big ideas, and so the country spoke through him like the breath blown through a flute. I love Auckland because of men like Bob. This matter of the censoring of *Craccum* (no doubt unimportant in itself) seems to me contrary to the spirit of Auckland as I have known it.

IRENE LIVED UNTIL 5 August 1976, when she died of pneumonia in Auckland Hospital. For a while after my father's death she had mysteriously lost the use of her legs, but rallied to complete her BA degree, majoring in English. After retirement from the law school library she remained active in voluntary work for such groups as the Citizens Association for Racial Equality (CARE), Citizens Advice Bureaux and Workers' Educational Association.

I sometimes went along to help her with envelope stuffing and mail-outs, though not often enough. I also got to know her better during late-night heart-to-hearts over the sherry-jar, when with my second baby Oliver I lived with her and young Brigid for a time at the One Tree Hill house before my marriage to Tom McWilliams. After we moved out of One Tree Hill, she and Brigid took a flat together; then, when Brigid moved on, Mum went to live in Sandringham with her friend Pat Dobbie.

In her last dreadful year my mother went downhill with what at first appeared a stroke, but was diagnosed as Korsakoff's Disease. Massive injections of Vitamin B came too late: her brain was shrivelled from alcoholic cerebral degenerative disease, her common sense gone. Her prolonged love affair with homebrew, Lemora, burgundy and dry sherry had become her undoing.

ROBIN, IRENE, BRIGID, JUDY WITH BABY TESSA MITCHELL, IN FRONT. VANYA WITH OLIVER : WADE 1967

LEFT: ALICE & BARRY McWILLIAMS
RIGHT: MURRAY GRIMSDALE,
IRENE & BRIGID, AT TOM & VANYA'S WEDDING, ABOVE, IN 1967

IRENE (LEFT) WITH VANYA & HER DIP. FINE ARTS 1967

Irene Lowry, B.A.

Even in the safety of a Fairview Road rest home, she was stroppy and would escape to wander up the street to the Mitchells, now living at number 4. Judy felt that Irene was ready to die when she was no longer interested in a proffered cigarette. Here's a poem of Brigid's about that time, entitled 'Irene':

Only the husk of you left,
all spark and flicker gone.
Violets and camellias in the resthome garden
no longer hold meaning,
don't light your tenantless eyes.
I show them to you anyway
and talk, words loud
over television, woven between
the close air, the tired and finished ladies
waiting neatly in cardigans for death.
Words and camellias anyway
in case you faintly feel them, want to know.
Bird in a winter tree, hear me.

When our mother went in to Auckland Hospital for the last time, I took my ten-month-old daughter, Amber, to visit and she happily explored under the strange bed. I remembered the last coherent words my mother had said to me: 'The best thing about dying is, you can eat as much as you like and never get fat . . .' But now Irene was barely breathing; there was blood on the pillow. She did not respond to my voice when I begged her to open her eyes and admire the lovely bouquet from her CARE colleagues. It was the last time I saw her.

An interesting story about our mother came to light recently. Janet Yiakmis, daughter of Irene's close friend Norah Dumble, had a Queenstown boarding-house. A friend named Margaret needed a bed for the night but the rooms were full. So Margaret was given Norah's bedroom in the place over the road. At the foot of Norah's bed hung the lovely Dennis Knight Turner portrait of Irene with a basket of fruit. In the morning Janet asked Margaret if she'd been comfortable. But Margaret said she was not able to get to sleep, not till she'd taken 'that lady's portrait' off the wall as she could not bear it looking at her. Fifteen minutes later my sister Judy phoned to say that Irene had died in the night.

AUCKLAND
WORKERS' EDUCATIONAL ASSOCIATION
INCORPORATED

1a PONSONBY ROAD AUCKLAND 1
10.30 — 2.30 DAILY MONDAY TO FRIDAY :: 769-664
ORGANIZING SECRETARY

19 August 1976

Ms Vanya Lowry
7 Burnley Terrace
MT EDEN 3.

Dear Vanya,

We were all deeply grieved at Irene's death. We feel that we have lost a friend and a most devoted supporter and worker.

To you who have suffered an even greater loss we extend our sympathy.

The Auckland WEA owes a great debt to Irene and we are glad that we were able to recognise this in a small way last year by making her an honorary life member.

However, we hope to be able to more suitably recognise her contributions to the causes that she served by the creation of some sort of annual award.

What we tentatively propose is the creation of a fund, in conjunction with Care and the Peace Foundation, to be known as the 'Irene Lowry Memorial Fund'. Money from the fund could be used each year to help subsidise the education of a Pacific Island or Maori student.

Alternatively, we could annually award a prize for the most useful contribution to race relations in New Zealand.

We hope that you will let us know what you think of this, as well as any other ideas that you may have toward a suitable memorial for Irene.

Yours sincerely,

John Colquhoun

for the DISTRICT COUNCIL and EXECUTIVE.

ONE FINE DAY recently, wandering along under the oaks on One Tree Hill, I stop beside the neat brick wall that my aunt Jessie's husband, Bill Sutton, had to finish after Daddy's suicide. Suddenly I find myself bravely pushing open the gate and walking firmly down the path beside the garage, where white anemones used to bloom and still do. I knock on the door and a friendly grey-haired man accepts my explanation that I lived my first twenty years in this house. The man, whose name is John, invites me in. Smiling, he explains that my three sisters have all visited over the years, and he and his wife were wondering when I might do the same. He kindly starts showing me around the rooms, asking if I know that the original house had been built for Captain Wynyard of the pioneering Auckland family.

It all seems much smaller than I remember, especially the Big Room, partly because I'm bigger, partly because of the tricks memory plays, and partly because the walls have been papered in fancy flocked wallpapers and these people have much more furniture than the Lowrys ever did. When John's wife, Pat, emerges from the Bedroom Wing, I apologise if I've woken her from a Sunday afternoon snooze. But she too is kind, and lets me admire the changes in the Bedroom Wing, where the cubicles are now small bedrooms. Then she takes me up the other end of the house, where now she creates quirky garden ornaments in what used to be our parents' bedroom and study. I'm given a welcome cup of tea and sit sipping it at a small kitchen table while she prepares vegetables for the evening's roast dinner, as they're expecting a visit from their daughter and her family.

John tells me there's an old painting tucked away in the garage and maybe I could see if I recognise it? I do. It's one of mine! The black rocks like rotten teeth amid swirling waves were my awful Bay of Islands series while at art school. These were the ones that made my poor painting teacher, Colin McCahon, advise me to 'stick to graphics'!

Strangely enough, I tell John and Pat, I'd given my first-born son, Wiri, up for adoption before beginning the series. And, though I didn't know where he'd gone, or why I'd started these strange lonely-looking paintings of a place I'd never been to, I found out at our reunion years later that Wiri (now named George) had spent his first few years in the Bay of Islands. My life is full of such coincidences.

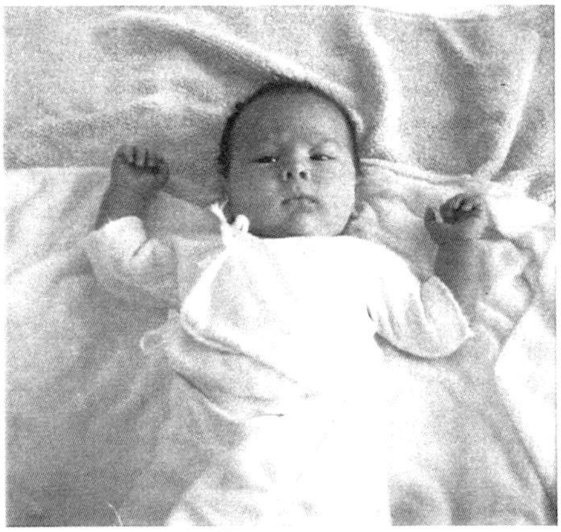

WIRI

Outside, there's now a rose garden where my father used to tend his vegetables. My wistaria bush is now a giant tree trailing over a huge trellis. The plum tree is now lichen-covered and dead-looking, apparently for the chop, no longer producing those luscious yellow plums every summer. I suppose Rex's choko vine choked it in the end. All the surviving plants have grown enormous in the years since that terrible day my father was left alone in the house. I was pregnant and becoming swollen with Wiri. And if there was some miraculous way to go back in time, that is the moment I would definitely choose. I'd accept the offer to marry Wiri's gorgeous creamcake father, who was such a bad influence on me, and I on him! But I would do it, if it meant I could stay at home and keep my darling Wiri. I would have looked after my husband and my baby and my father and the house I loved. And maybe Daddy would not have died if one of us could have stayed.

I know what's done can't be undone. But if only I had known, had some idea of the depths of my father's despair. My mother never told us, because she *had* to leave for her own survival, and of course had to take ten-year-old Brigid. As for me, at twenty, I was the only one who could possibly have stayed, and I should not have abandoned him . . .

BUT THIS OLD house at One Tree Hill was such a marvellous place to grow up in. Sure, our parents left us to our own devices a lot of the time. I think it was because they struggled to make sense of their own lives and commitments, as well as struggling to make ends meet, and struggling to deal with the results of their belief in utopia, socialism and 'free love' (which I happen to think does not exist).

Yet they gave me what they could — so much, really! Our father's vegetable garden provided bounty; we had fruit trees, swings and climbing trees, plus the Park at our gate. Our mother bottled fruit, made wholesome bread and cottage cheese, conserved guava jelly, marmalade ... we were so *healthy*! She stretched the budget so I could have a pair of shoes after the Bullyboys hid mine up a puriri tree. More than once she bought me a new dress (I remember one for the Queen's visit in 1953). From her I gained my philosophical streak, plus an awareness of, and deep love for, poetry and classical music. She taught me the value of honesty, and usefulness, why we should care about 'the suffering millions' out in the world as well as closer to home. My father was proud of us and, apart from recipes for then unusual things like yoghurt (he made his own) and capers (he made 'poor man's capers' from homegrown nasturtium seeds), he bequeathed his love of books and language and art and typography, and an eye for design detail (such as the niceties of poster design), and things as simple as how to sharpen a good pencil which I've never forgotten. Also, of course, the gift of that marvellous whimsical Irish humour, although I could never master his knack of telling a joke and remembering the punchline!

Now, on my visit back to One Tree Hill, as well as the old Bay of Islands painting (to which I will add some 'improvements' of golden sun and happy birds), I carry away gifts of grapefruit from our old tree and a tamarillo from a new tree down the track. Walking down to the bus stop, my gladness is tinged with sadness at the way things worked out.

So relinquish me, house, for you are my yesterday.

DAVID MITCHELL (CENTRE) IN MICK JAGGER DISGUISE
WITH SISTERS-IN-LAW VANYA (LEFT) & BRIGID

ACKNOWLEDGEMENTS

I would like to thank the editors of AUP's *Big Smoke* poetry anthology for including some of my 'fragments', which gave me strength to finish *From the Wistaria Bush*, and in a roundabout way led to its publication; also my Readers (who know who they are) for encouragement; the lads at Copy it in Colour on Broadway for their cheerful lasering of so much visual material; Annie and Christine at the friendly AUP office; my editor Andrew Mason; typesetter Katrina Duncan, and publisher Elizabeth Caffin.

To those who gave permissions, my thanks. Reasonable effort has been made to clear copyrights; if you were missed, please contact the publisher, AUP, in case of future editions. Credits for photos and artworks are as follows:

p. v	Bob, Vanya, Irene, Robin, Judy, Pop. © George Cornes Estate.
p. vi	Honey drawing. V.L.
p. ix	Irene. © Clifton Firth Estate.
p. x	Irene and 'Pudding'; Vanya during water scarcity. © Cornes Estate.
p. 1	Vanya and Irene. © Cornes Estate.
p. 2	New Caledonia and Solomons. © Lowry Estate.
p. 4	Lowrys' Christmas card. Design © Elspeth Hitchings Estate.
p. 6	Robin, Judy and Vanya. © Cornes Estate.
p. 9	Bob in his beloved garden. Photo collage. V.L.
p. 11	Head of Bob. © Eric Lee-Johnson Estate.
p. 14–15	Mead recipe. © Norah Dumble Estate.
p. 17	The big bedroom. Photo collage. V.L.
p. 18	Girl, sun & butterflowers. V.L.
p. 20	Title page of *Biscotti and Caramelle*. Drawing by Molly Macalister.
p. 23	Vanya and Bill Anso. Street photographer.
p. 25	The big room. © Cornes Estate.
p. 26	9 Clifton Rd; Pop and Gran. © Althea Northey.
p. 27	Ellison Chambers. © *Auckland Star*.
p. 28	Percy family tree. V.L.
p. 31	Brontosaurus stomp. © Robert Brett.
p. 32-33	'Abbreviated Bill of Foodstuffs' in honour of visit of poets from the South, devised by Irene and Bob Lowry, Pat Dobbie, and Rex Fairburn.
p. 35	Party fare drawing. V.L.
p. 37	From *The Sky is a Limpet*. Text © A.R.D. Fairburn Estate.
p. 38	Bob with Venus under the plum tree. V.L.
p. 40	Vanya, Judy and Robin; Robin in brown velvet. © Cornes Estate.
p. 43	Butterscotch recipe, written by Irene; Puddings drawing. V.L.
p. 45	Old Maharajah. © Pat Dobbie Estate; Bob. © Bells Camera House, Wellington.
p. 48	Vanya aged about nine. Street Photographer.
p. 51	Vanya swimming.
p. 55	Sleeping girl and wistaria collage. V.L.
p. 56	Bob as a child. © Lesnie, Paeroa.

Estate; Plum-wine drawing. V.L.

p. 122 Lowry family Christmas card with William Jones drawing; drawing of Rex Fairburn. V.L.

p. 123 Invitation to wayzgoose; clipping on Pilgrim Press; Ron Holloway note quoting Glover.

p. 124 Bob's jobbing book.

p. 125 Painting of Bob. © Dennis Knight Turner.

p. 126 Wayzgoose at Pilgrim Press. © Robin Lush.

p. 127 One-eyed King and Gertrude. © Clifton Firth Estate.

p. 128–9 Bob's show at Elam. V.L.

p. 131 Bob at Airedale Street. © Robin Lush.

p. 132 Christmas card with whale and ship.

p. 134 Irene and Vanya, old (photographer unknown) and young (© Cornes Estate).

p. 137 Drawing, Bob's gravestone. V.L.

p. 138 *Auckland Star* obituary.

p. 143 Robin, Irene, Brigid, Judy with Tessa, Vanya with Oliver, 1967. © Simon Buis Estate.

p. 144 Vanya's wedding, 1967. © Roger Donaldson.

p. 145 Vanya's graduation. © Simon Buis Estate.

p. 146 Irene's graduation. © Simon Buis Estate.

p. 147 Camellia drawing. V.L.

p. 148 Irene and fruit painting. © Dennis Knight Turner.

p. 149 WEA letter.

p. 150 Painting, Bay of Islands. V.L.

p. 151 Wiri. © William Henry Port Estate.

p. 153 One Tree Hill house. © Cornes Estate.

p. 154 Circling bird drawing. V.L.; David Mitchell and sisters-in-law. © Simon Buis Estate.

p. 158 Vanya, Judy and Robin in party mode. © Cornes Estate; One Tree Hill in the 1950s. V.L.

Excerpts came from the following sources: *Hot Water Sailor*, © Denis Glover Estate; *Book 8*, August 1948, © Denis Glover Estate; 'Remembering Bob Lowry', *Landfall*, vol. 69, March 1964, © Ron Holloway/Caxton Press; 'On a Dilatory Printer', *Cold Tongue*, 1940, © Denis Glover Estate/Caxton Press; 'Poem addressed to Mr Robert Lowry on the Occasion of the Birth of his Fourth Daughter', *Poetry Harbinger*, 1958, © Rex Fairburn Estate/Pilgrim Press; 'The Ballad of One Tree Hill' and 'Auckland', *Collected Poems, James K. Baxter*, Oxford University Press, 1979, © James K. Baxter Estate; 'Remembering the Wade', *Landfall*, © Michael Jackson/Caxton Press; 'Grotesques', *Kiwi*, 1965, © Kendrick Smithyman Estate; 'I Remember Bob Lowry', *Craccum*, May 1964, © James K. Baxter Estate; 'Irene' poem, © Brigid Lowry.

One Tree Hill in the 50s

Vanya, Judy, Robin in party mode